Sell It Yourself As FSBO

An Insider's Roadmap to Selling Your Home and Saving on Commissions

Veronica Silva

ISBN: 9798862218046

Printed by KDP Publishing, an Amazon company. Printed in the United States of America.

DISCLAIMER

The author has strived to be as accurate and complete as possible in the creation of this book. This book and any companion manual and course is designed to provide information on selling homes and residential real estate in general. It is sold with the understanding that neither the author nor the publisher is engaged in rendering legal, accounting or other professional services or advice. If legal or other professional services are warranted, the reader is encouraged to seek the advice of an attorney and any other professional and retain the services of any such professional as they may deem fit. **The information contained in this book, accompanying manuals and or related courses is strictly for education purposes only. Any reader who applies the information contained in this book, accompanying manual and/or related courses assumes full responsibility for their actions.** While the author has made every effort to present complete and accurate information, this book may contain errors or omissions and the information may become outdated and therefore inaccurate by marketplace or industry changes or conditions, new laws or regulations, or other circumstances. The author and publisher make no representation or warranties with respect to the accuracy, applicability, fitness or completeness of the information contained in this book, any accompanying manuals and or related course, nor make any promise regarding achievable results. **The information may not be suitable for every situation.** Neither the author nor the publisher accepts any responsibility or liability to any person or entity with respect to any loss or damage alleged to have been caused, directly or indirectly, by the information, ideas, opinions or other content in this book and any related manual and/or course. **While the author is a licensed real estate agent in the State of Illinois, and a licensed attorney (currently inactive) in the State of Illinois, the author has not established either an agency relationship or an attorney-client relationship with any and all readers of this book, any accompanying manual and/or related course participant.** The author is not providing neither legal nor real estate advice. The information and opinions expressed by the author are solely hers and do not reflect the opinions or approval of the brokerage the author is currently affiliated with, has been affiliated with in the past, or may be affiliated with in the future after the publishing of this book. **If you do not agree to these terms, you should return this book for a full refund immediately but no later than 5 business days from the date of purchase.**

ABOUT THE AUTHOR

Prior to becoming a real estate agent, Veronica Silva studied law in South America and in the U.S. earning her J.D. and Master of Law degrees from the University of Pennsylvania in 2001 and 2003. She practiced law at two of the top 10 law firms in the country and at a labor and employment boutique prior to opening her own law firm. **Her legal career covered a total of fifteen years combined before she transitioned to residential real estate.** She started her real estate career at Keller Williams and is currently affiliated with  Coldwell Banker Realty (2023). She is fluent in Spanish and English and is passionate about helping people with their real estate needs. The skills she developed as an attorney have become her secret weapon when representing clients as a real estate agent. She is a member of the National Association of Realtors and the Mainstreet Organization of Realtors of Illinois. She believes in striving for excellence and upholding the highest level of integrity. She believes in elevating and empowering the people around her with information for everyone to be able to confidently and freely make their own decisions.

She sold her own house as FSBO in 2012 and many other homes as an agent since 2019. Read the full story in the Foreword in this book.

TABLE OF CONTENTS

ACKNOWLEDGEMENTS

I would first like to thank all of **YOU** who have taken the step to get this book in your hands. The decision you made to lean-in and be curious enough to learn tells me that you are a smart and motivated individual who strives to do the right thing for yourself. I hope this book brings you value and enables you in your success!

I would also like to acknowledge a few people who have greatly contributed to, and influenced, my growth and development. Without their guidance I would not be where I am today writing this book. I may know some of them personally and others have been dear mentors to me without their knowledge, but extremely impactful nonetheless. It is through the great work they have created and shared with the world that I have learned the importance of a growth mindset. Let me start with **Gary Keller, founder of Keller Williams Realty**. Without being part of Keller Williams at the start of my career, I would not have gained the awareness of what is possible to achieve and give back in this greatly challenging but equally fulfilling field. I am beyond grateful for your books "The Millionaire Real Estate Agent" and "Shift". They have been the foundation for my career. Next is **Pete Economos**, operating partner of several Keller Williams market centers in the Chicagoland area, whose words of wisdom, business acumen and market insights have taught me how to become a sophisticated residential real estate agent and consultant. I strongly believe that learning from him significantly differentiates me from most other real estate professionals. To **Robert Rohm, Ph.D.**, and his book Positive Personality Profiles - thank you for giving me the gift of understanding myself and most importantly of accepting my personality traits. Thanks to the knowledge you shared I no longer feel like there is something wrong with me for constantly desiring change, needing to grow every day, and for always wanting much more out of life (I am a high D and C - if you know, you know). To **Keith J. Cunningham** and his book The Road Less Stupid filled with so much great advice to become a high level thinker and fully step into the role of business owner. To **James Clear** and his book Atomic Habits, for giving me back the self-discipline I had lost somehow in the busy years of raising little children and always putting others first. To **Brian P. Moran and Michael Lennington,** for their book the 12 Week Year, which gave me the tools to recover from a period of several years (that just seemed to have evaporated) without much being accomplished. To the late **coach Borino,** who was taken from this world way too soon. His even keeled approach and kindness left a lasting mark on me, as I am sure was also the case for many of his students. He was generous with his knowledge and we could all feel he truly cared. I still think of his lessons and carry them with me. I hope his family is doing well and I hope they find comfort in knowing that he positively impacted so many lives. To **John Carlson,** for our weekly check-ins as Coldwell Banker Realty's Managing Broker (Naperville, IL office). Thank you for your time, insights and overall great positive outlook and perspectives.

More personally, to **my children A and O** for keeping me on my toes and giving me the drive to keep going no matter what happens. I am grateful I got to be the mom of such good kids back then and to now have the most delightful teenagers. I treasure you, even in those days where your "teenagery" shows up with intensity. It gives me great joy to see you both grow up and become your own person. To **my**

brother Emiliano and his wife Adriana for the endless support and encouragement and for being trusted advisors in all things "life" with brilliant insights. You are doing a wonderful job as parents to **V. and M.** and I greatly admire you for it. To my **parents Roque and Mirta,** for raising me in a stable loving home, always striving to make thoughtful parenting decisions and instilling in me such a strong moral compass. To my **dear friend Erika T.,** I am grateful for your authentic and honest friendship which I treasure with all my heart. Your strength to keep on going inspires me everyday. Last but certainly not least, to **Alastair** - words cannot describe how grateful I am that you came into my life. Thank you for the immense grace you have shown me, at the beginning, and ever since. You are not only wicked smart, but also just about the strongest man in character and integrity I have ever known. Your endless kindness, selflessness, ironclad commitment and unwavering loyalty have built me back up again in more ways than you will ever know. I feel deeply loved and happy because of you and I can only hope that, at a bare minimum, I can make you feel just as loved and happy. Thank you for supporting me in this book project… emotionally, brainstorming ideas, and with practical hands-on help. I could not have done it without you.

FOREWORD

It was the Spring of 2012 - This single mom with two little ones under 6 years old had already tried to sell her marital home located in Glenview, IL the previous Spring of 2011 but it just sat on the market for months and months until she ended up taking it off the market by the winter. When Spring came again, it was time for her to make a decision about selling the property. At the time, it was the aftermath of the 2008 real estate bubble bursting. Every month that went by her house was worth less and less and she could see all her equity evaporating. How did she get herself into that situation? This single mom was a professional with a legal career. She and her ex-husband had purchased the house for $700,000 at the peak of the market in 2007 and immediately had added about $50,000 in renovating the master bedroom and bathroom. Yes, the market was turning but who cares, they thought, as they planned to live there for the rest of their lives and there was plenty of time for home values to recover after the recession. Little did they know that despite the joy of a new house, and a second baby coming to complete their family, the marriage would soon be in trouble and in just 4 years she would be faced with needing to sell the house. Between the down payment and the renovations, over $190,000 of savings they had invested in the house were on the line. As a newly divorced single mother, whatever equity she could get out of the house sale would be essential to the new phase of her life that was just beginning. Getting the most equity out of that house was vital to her future and the future of her children. The sale was inevitable, but how could she protect her equity in a spiraling market?

When she tried to sell it in the Spring of 2011 she had hired an agent from a popular brokerage with plenty of years of experience and a big team behind him. After many months of being on the market in 2011, the house would not sell and each month that went by felt like she was sinking deeper and deeper into a financial hole along with each price reduction she had to agree to do, hoping that it would bring an offer and end the nightmare. The mortgage payments were huge and even though she was a successful lawyer with a stable job, she was now a single income household. She had to sell it ASAP yet the market was on shaky grounds and, as experienced as the team of real estate agents she had hired was, they were not able to navigate the shifting market and advise her in a way that would save her equity and protect her from the financial ruin awaiting at the end of the tunnel.

It was now time to list it for sale again (in the Spring of 2012) and all she could think of was the failure of the previous Spring. After much thought and consideration she decided to list it "For Sale By Owner" (FSBO) to save on commissions and that way salvage some of the equity that was still in the house. While she was a busy professional with two little children to care for, she felt she had no choice - it was either trying to sell as FSBO or giving up the little equity she had left in the house. In the end, she sold it and was able to at least recover $40,000 in equity (and if you feel inclined to do a little math, go ahead...but here is a spoiler alert - she lost $150,000 worth of equity). When all was said and done, she was relieved and happy she had decided to try the FSBO route and did not think much about it...for a while at least...but well, that single mother was...ME! I am telling you the details of this chapter of my life because I want you to **believe me when I say...I can totally**

understand why a homeowner would try to sell as FSBO. I have certainly been in most FSBOs' shoes when it comes to saving your hard earned money and savings and being mindful of not wasting any of it. Isn't that the main reason why you listed it for-sale-by-owner? In my experience, that is the main reason most FSBOs claim not to hire an agent.

Fast forward several years later…I became a real estate agent in 2019. I quit my legal career and decided to become a Realtor™! Let me tell you that after doing real estate for over 4 years, I can look back and see how many mistakes I made in 2012 as a FSBO! Oh my! Do I wish I could have had back then at least a few of the many resources available today for selling as FSBO! The internet was still in its rather early stages in 2012 if you compare it to what it is today… And social media? Facebook is all I knew back then and it was just becoming popular mainly as a way to reconnect with old friends from high school. Facebook was definitely not being used for commerce and business that much over a decade ago. At the time, all I had at my disposal was my previous experience of trying to sell it with an agent the year before, and a law degree. The legal expertise was certainly useful to comfortably navigate most of the paperwork. I really don't know how much harder it would have been to do it all if I didn't have at least my legal background skills. Luckily, I am a very observant person and because of my legal career, I have a highly developed attention to detail skill set. This allowed me to soak all the insights and steps of the listing process that the team of agents I hired followed in 2011. I basically copied as much as I could what they had done the previous year. However, I will be the first to admit that if I had not gone through the listing process with those professionals the year before, I would have been completely clueless and helpless in terms of preparing the house for sale and doing some minimal marketing to promote the listing. Preparing the house for sale is one of the tasks in the sales process that the majority of FSBOs find to be the most difficult. By the same token, I will be the first to admit that I probably left money on the table (or to be more precise, money in the buyer's pockets) because I had no way of gathering real time market data to price my home. Also, I did not know much about negotiating in real estate sales. I surely had negotiating experience as an attorney, but I couldn't be as effective as the buyers' agents in negotiating a real estate sale. I cannot help but think how much more successful I could have been in the sale of my home as FSBO had I had a bit more knowledge and understanding of the real estate sales process. Of course as they say, looking back hindsight is always 20/20…One other huge factor that I had completely overlooked was the fact that - I was too close to the transaction! Even with my legal training, I could not be as objective as professional agents. After becoming an agent myself I got to learn (and experience first hand) the significant difference that it makes when negotiations are led by professionals who are detached from the property, both financially and emotionally. Did you know that when real estate agents have to sell their own homes they will ask for help from a colleague and have them co-list with them and run the negotiations? You would be surprised how common this practice is.

Today, I have developed laser vision and focus, after growing my skills and gaining experience as a professional real estate agent. ***Plus, having lived through the sale of real estate as a FSBO, I am in a unique position to share my knowledge and experience with***

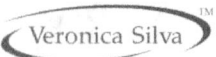
others. **That is why I am writing this book!** *I want to share all that I have learned as a FSBO back then, and as an agent now, to save homeowners from making the mistakes I made because I did not know any better.* **That is the purpose of putting together this book!** <u>*I want everyone who is thinking of selling their house to know more than I did when I had to sell mine in 2011. I want every potential seller out there to know really what it will take to sell as FSBO and what are the risks lurking in the shadows and the rewards awaiting at the end of the tunnel.*</u> I want everyone who may be considering selling as FSBO to know so much more than I did, before making the decision to go at it alone. **I want everyone considering a real estate sale without an agent to make an informed decision fully aware of what they are getting into.** I believe to my core that in everything in life, when you know more, you can achieve more! Only those who know better can do better. <u>So here is this roadmap for all my fellow homeowners who are brave enough to even consider selling their home as FSBO.</u> This guide is meant to help you make a wise choice with confidence, considering all the relevant factors, so you never have to second guess yourself because you did what was best for you! And if you decide to go for it, I want you to know that I am rooting for you and that I encourage you to learn as much as you can before and during the sale. Never stop analyzing and researching. **<u>As a FSBO, you are the underdog, and I am rooting for you to end up with a successful outcome!</u>** **I want you to be proud of the end result because you have reached your goals! GO GET THEM!**

CHAPTER 1 - INTRODUCTION: WHY SELL REAL ESTATE AS A FOR SALE BY OWNER?

1. INTRODUCTION TO SELLING REAL ESTATE AS A "FOR SALE BY OWNER" (OR "FSBO")

Real estate is not only one of the largest purchases most average adults will make, but also has the potential to be one of the most lucrative investments that anyone can make. A real estate asset can yield significant returns, not only because of its value appreciation overtime, but also because of tax deductions related to owning real estate. This explains why about two thirds of an individual's net worth comes from holding equity in real estate. Homeownership is the main source of wealth for most Americans. If you don't believe this, all you have to do is search online for multiple sources of this information. When it comes to selling real estate, most people turn to real estate agents for help (92% of real estate sales are completed using a real estate agent according to the National Association of Realtors). However, with the increasing availability of technology and online resources, more people than ever before are now considering selling their property as a For Sale By Owner (FSBO), either to save money on commissions and fees, or sometimes, solely because they perceive they have more control of the process and terms of sale, if they sell their property as a FSBO.

A FSBO sale is where the property owner sells their property without the services of a real estate agent representing the seller side of the transaction. In a FSBO sale, the owner takes on the role of a seller's real estate agent and manages all aspects of the sale process that a seller's agent would manage, including property preparation, pricing, marketing, showings, negotiations, completing legal paperwork, etc. A FSBO can

also accept or reject working with a real estate agent representing the buyers. Also, a FSBO can agree to compensate the buyer's real estate agent or not. Agreeing to compensate a buyer's agent and agreeing to a buyer having their own agent representing them, are two separate issues. If a FSBO does not want to compensate the buyer's agent, the buyers themselves will need to compensate their own agent which will be paid out of their own pockets and not included in the purchase price of the home.

While the process of selling real estate may seem daunting at first, selling real estate as a FSBO is an excellent way to both save money and to gain more control over the sales process. In this chapter, we will explore the benefits and drawbacks of selling real estate as a FSBO and help you understand the role of real estate agents and why some sellers choose to sell by themselves.

2. BENEFITS OF SELLING REAL ESTATE AS A FSBO

One of the main benefits of selling real estate as a FSBO is the cost savings. Real estate agents typically charge a commission (in most cases) anywhere from 2 to 9% of the sale price (combined between seller's agent and buyer's agent commissions). Commission paid by the seller is negotiable in most states and you may be able to negotiate any commission percentage (or even a fixed dollar amount) with the agent who will represent you. Regardless of the percentage or fixed fee, commissions can amount to many thousands of dollars. By selling the property as a FSBO, the seller can avoid paying any commission whatsoever, or at a minimum, avoid paying the seller's agent commission (while still paying the buyer's agent commission) and keep more of the profits from the sale for themselves. Most FSBOs come to realize during the sales process that if they do not offer to pay the buyer's agent commission themselves, the number of potentially interested buyers is greatly reduced. <u>Do not forget that buyers' agents are instrumental in bringing **serious** potential buyers to see properties available for sale.</u>

Another benefit of selling real estate as a FSBO is the increased control over the sales process. This should not be misinterpreted as the seller not having decision power or control over the sales process when working with an agent, including which offer they accept or reject. What this means is that when working with a real estate agent, the seller often has limited control over how the property is marketed, who is shown the property, and how negotiations are managed. By selling the property as a FSBO, the seller can tailor the sales process more narrowly to their specific needs and preferences, resulting in a more personalized sales experience. But regardless of whether sellers hire an agent to represent them or not, the seller always has the final word as to which price and terms of sale they accept. In most states, licensed real estate agents are not able to make decisions on behalf of their clients. They lack legal authority to call the shots of the sale. The owner/seller is the decision-maker and has all the power to make such decisions. The role of a real estate agent is discussed in more detail later in this chapter.

3. DRAWBACKS OF SELLING REAL ESTATE AS A FSBO

While there are many benefits to selling real estate as a FSBO, there are also some drawbacks to consider. One of the biggest drawbacks is the time and effort required to sell the property. Selling real estate requires dedicating a significant amount of time and attention, and for those who have other commitments, such as work or family, this can be challenging.

Another potential drawback of selling real estate as a FSBO is the lack of expertise and experience. Real estate agents have years of experience and knowledge of the market, as well as access to a vast network of potential buyers. Without this expertise and network, selling the property can be even more challenging and time-consuming for a FSBO than it would be for a real estate agent. Recognizing that as a FSBO you likely lack the expertise, tools and experience real estate professionals have in their favor, is an important first step. Any FSBO would be wise to acknowledge and accept this gap that puts them at a disadvantage (especially during the marketing and negotiation stages) so that he or she can minimize that disadvantage. A smart FSBO will dedicate a significant amount of time and effort prior to putting their house on the market to research and learn as much as possible about the process of selling real estate. A savvy FSBO will research which tools and resources real estate agents have and use daily, and put extra effort in procuring as much as possible similar tools and resources for themselves, even if they do not have a license. The National Association of Realtors 2020 Profile of Home Buyers and Sellers states that FSBOs list (1) Preparing the home for sale (Chapter 2), (2) completing the paperwork (Chapter 3) and (3) pricing the home correctly (Chapter 2) as the 3 most difficult tasks for them in the sale of their homes.

Finally, FSBOs need to be particularly aware that they have a subjective view of their property and they would be wise to make every effort to counter their subjective view with objective data and assessment. The typical phrase real estate agents hear from their seller clients is - "but there is no other home as special/nice/large/updated as mine" - and that belief can really hurt a seller because every buyer that considers your home is very likely to love another home just as much. Once you list your property for sale, it no longer is your "home" but has instead become a "house". In other words, your home becomes a commodity. Buyers will look at it that way and you should too.

"A commodity is a basic good used in commerce that is interchangeable with other goods of the same type."

4. THE ROLE OF REAL ESTATE AGENTS

Selling a property as a FSBO is a viable alternative that can save sellers money and provide more control over the sales process. But real estate agents play a crucial role in real estate transactions, regardless of whether they represent the seller or the buyer side of the deal.

Real estate professionals provide valuable services such as counseling sellers and buyers, marketing the property, valuing, and pricing the property, negotiating, and coordinating paperwork and making sure that all the different individuals who have other roles in the transaction such as inspectors, lenders, attorneys, appraisers, etc. execute their duties in a timely manner for the transaction to reach a successful closing.

Real estate agents are experts in the industry and can guide sellers (or buyers) through the sales process, providing valuable insights and advice and also have a huge role in keeping emotions at bay. It is very common for buyers and sellers to get anxious and nervous during the transaction and if emotions are let to run free, the process can go off rails and the transaction will fall apart, hurting everyone involved. Agents are professionals who can remain calm and keep everyone's goals in mind. The industry inside joke is that real estate agents are often called to play the role of therapists.

Finally, there is a popular public perception that real estate agents are generously compensated (or overly compensated), but this perception does not take into account the fact that most agents run their own businesses and are independent contractors, working 100% based on commissions and incurring business expenses and losses. Further, in many cases, the number of hours required from an agent to attend to a specific transaction is grossly underestimated. This is usually the case because most of the work a real estate agent does is performed behind the scenes and not really visible to the buyer and seller. Nevertheless, working with a real estate agent can be costly, and some sellers may prefer to sell their property without an agent to save money on commissions and fees. Regardless of whether you feel confident that you do not need an agent to sell your home, do not ever forget that most buyers will prefer to work with an agent and not directly with the seller. **A 2022 study by the National Association of Realtors revealed that**

86% of buyers worked with an agent when they were looking to buy a home, and only about 10% of them dealt directly with the seller/owner. About 2% bought from a builder and the remaining 2% of buyers found homes in some other manner. <u>The more serious a buyer is, the more certain you can be that they will be working with an agent.</u> These statistics should make you realize how important it is for you to market your property to attract agents, not just the buyers. And the more agent-like you conduct yourself, the more likely you will be to achieve your goals. Do not make the mistake of ignoring the way agents do business. You must learn it and match it, otherwise you are just swimming against the current, and no fish can reach their destination swimming against the current.

5. WHAT TO EXPECT OUT OF THIS BOOK AND PLAN THE TIMELINE FOR THE SALE

When it comes to this type of book, you will be hard pressed to find one that is written with a balanced and fair approach, without taking a position one way or the other and having "an agenda" behind it. In my experience, most of the books written about selling by owner are written by agents and other people in the real estate industry only to fulfill their own goals. You will find books on both sides of the aisle: some go hard on trying to convince you that selling by owner is super easy and that you only need common sense. These are usually written by someone who has a company that targets people willing to go the FSBO route, to sell them products to use during the FSBO sale (for example, selling them marketing products and advertising); while other authors take the opposite view that selling by owner is pretty much impossible or the dumbest thing you can do (clearly they want to discourage you from selling by yourself and steer you towards hiring an agent - or better said, hiring THEM as your agent). These are usually written by agents. *But this book will do neither.* Throughout the writing of this book my aim has been to present you with facts and knowledge every step of the way, so that you can be well informed and make your own decision as to which route – either selling as FSBO or hiring an agent – *will be the better way to go for you.* **This is a very personal choice. Both methods of selling real estate work, if done well. Likewise, both methods can fail or fall short, if poorly executed.**

Only you can make the determination of which path suits you, and your situation, best. You must decide for yourself if what's required of you to sell as a FSBO is something you are able and willing to give or get yourself into. Be suspicious of anyone giving you strong opinions one way or the other. If anyone is pushing you strongly for one option over the other, you will be wise to ask yourself - what is behind such a strong position? What does this person have at stake in my decision? **It really shouldn't be any of their business to persuade you one way or the other, or what you decide to do in the end.**

In order to get the most out of this book, I would suggest that you first do a quick read through to gain some general understanding of the sales process and check with yourself if that's something you want to get into. Whether going at it as a FSBO or not would be the first decision you will need to make. Once you make the decision to sell by owner instead of hiring an agent, you will need to read through this book a second time going step-by-step through each chapter in more detail, and doing the work for each stage of the sales process before moving on to the next chapter. I organized the chapters chronologically in the order that I have seen works best for prioritizing your tasks. Depending on the condition of your home, and the free time you have available to dedicate to the sale, you may need anywhere from just a few days to a full week to prepare your house (Chapter 2) but in some cases you may need as long as 3-6 weeks. I would say that based on experience, the average homeowner, who has done the average level of maintenance of the home while living in it, and who owns an average amount of belongings, will probably need 2-4 weeks of diligently dedicating about 5-7 hours per week to prepare the home for sale plus a full day worth of work each weekend. You may be wondering what is "average" - I would say that if most of your family and friends have a similar amount of belongings - you probably fall within the average range. However, if when you visit your family's and friends' homes you find them to be more "organized" or "tidy" and "empty" or "clutter-free" than yours, that's probably a sign that your home will require a bit more prep time than the average. Next is to fully comprehend the paperwork (Chapter 3). Again, depending on how much prior knowledge you have of the laws and regulations of your state, you may need more or less time to get a handle of the documents that you will need. On average, a FSBO will need about 4-6 hours focused on researching, gathering and reviewing the paperwork to get started. As soon as the house is ready for viewing, and you have completed the disclosures required in your state, then you can put your marketing plan into action (Chapter 4). Implementing the marketing plan will be an ongoing task until you accept an offer and your house goes "under contract" or "pending." The

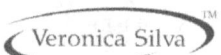

market conditions in your area will greatly determine how long you will need to maintain your marketing efforts going. You can figure out what to expect by noticing how long do houses usually stay "active" for sale on the market before they go "pending." Once you unleash your marketing plan, you will be busy with showings and open houses (Chapter 5). Once again, depending on the market conditions you may be very busy with multiple private showings each week, or they may come like rain drops. One thing is certain - you will experience the heaviest load of requests for showings in the initial week or two of going on the market. After this initial period, it always slows down. Don't get discouraged, this is normal. Once you receive an offer (Chapter 6), the negotiation process may take from a few hours to a couple of days depending on the number of sale terms that you need to agree upon. Normal negotiations do not extend over more than a couple of days. If a buyer does not respond to you within a day or so, they may have lost interest and moved on to the next property. Keep this in mind and be diligent in your communications during negotiations of an offer. Finally, when you are approaching the closing of the sale you will have already prepared most of the paperwork and will have the assistance of a title company for the final steps (Chapter 7). There are a few other tips towards the end of this book on how to deal with difficult buyers (Chapter 8) and key takeaways from the book (Chapter 10). Finally, in case you decide that selling as FSBO is not the way to go for you, you will find tips on how to select a real estate agent at the end (Chapter 9).

6. CONCLUSION

Selling real estate as a FSBO can be an excellent way to save money and gain more control over the sales process but do not make the mistake of believing that it will be free or effortless. While there are some drawbacks to consider, for many sellers the benefits of selling real estate as a FSBO outweigh the negative aspects. In the following chapters, we will explore the steps and best practices for selling real estate as a FSBO.

CHAPTER 2 - PREPARING YOUR PROPERTY FOR SALE: TIPS AND BEST PRACTICES

Preparing your property for sale is an essential step in the sales process. The goal is to make your property as attractive as possible to potential buyers while maximizing its value. This chapter will cover some of the essential steps to take when preparing your property for sale as a FSBO.

1. REPAIRS AND UPGRADES

Assessing your property's condition and making necessary repairs and upgrades is a crucial preliminary step in preparing your property for sale. A well-maintained and updated property will attract many more potential buyers and the higher demand will result in a higher sale price. Follow these simple steps to fully assess your property.

1) **Assess your house's condition:** Take a thorough walk-through of your home and assess its condition. Look for any repairs that need to be made, such as leaky faucets, cracked tiles, scratched flooring, scuffed walls, trim or cabinets, or chipped paint, misaligned doors, etc. Make sure to write down the items needing your attention listing them room-by-room as items tend to add up quickly and it will become overwhelming. ***Check out the helpful checklists in the companion guide to this book.***

2) **Prioritize repairs:** Once you have identified repairs that need to be made, prioritize them based on their importance and cost. Focus on making necessary repairs first, such as fixing plumbing

or electrical issues, before making cosmetic upgrades. This is important because these types of repairs will most certainly be flagged by a home inspector hired by whoever is buying your home. Also, any items that are in a state of disrepair (like a leaky faucet or a stain in the ceiling from an old leak) will immediately raise concerns in the minds of buyers making them fearful that you did not adequately maintain the home. This usually makes buyers be afraid of what else could be wrong with the house that is not yet apparent. Keep in mind that you do not have to spend a lot of money on these improvements. Small improvements can make a significant difference in the overall look and feel of your property.

3) **Consider upgrades:** Only after having taken care of repairs should you consider making upgrades to your property to increase its appeal to potential buyers. Upgrades such as new appliances, updated light fixtures, contemporary fans, new carpets, and fresh paint can add a lot of value and appeal and make your property more attractive. When making these upgrades, you must consider the price point of your home. It always backfires when sellers replace appliances, light fixtures or plumbing fixtures with something new, but of lower grade that does not match the property's price point. For example, if your home is in the middle price point in your area, you should not be buying the lowest grade, or most economical simple appliances. Go for the middle grade, or slightly higher. In my experience, the differences in price will be more than made up in the final sales price. I have seen it happen many times, when

sellers install the cheapest ($300-$500) dishwasher or a gas range, in a home that is priced slightly higher than the middle price point homes in the area. This mistake will be costly in terms of timely selling the home for the highest possible price. Buyers in each price point have certain expectations when it comes to the quality of finishes and the grade of appliances that go on par with the price point of the home.

4) **Set a budget:** Set a budget for repairs and upgrades and stick to it. It is important to balance the cost of repairs and upgrades with the potential increase in sale price. The biggest return on investment in terms of upgrades in preparation for a sale is PAINT. ***Check out the helpful list of return on investment per update in the companion guide to this book.***

5) **Get professional advice:** If you feel lost, consider hiring a local contractor, handyman, or real estate agent to help you assess your property's condition and make recommendations of repairs and upgrades that will bring you the highest value and return.

2. CLEAN AND DECLUTTER YOUR HOME

Another essential step in preparing your home before listing it for sale, is to clean and declutter it. A cluttered or dirty property is a huge turnoff to potential buyers, and it makes your home look smaller. It can also make it difficult for potential buyers to visualize themselves living in the space. Start decluttering your home by getting rid of any unnecessary items, such as old furniture, clothes, and other knick knacks. Remove all personal items (e.g. family portraits and travel souvenirs, etc.) and art or decor that is too unique. Think of higher end hotels - they are usually decorated in a very neutral color palette and decor, including wall art. That's the look you want to replicate. You can look at pictures of hotels online (think Sheraton, Hyatt, Marriott, etc.) to give you an idea of which styles are currently popular. Next, give your home a deep clean, including the floors, walls, and any other surfaces. Make sure to pay attention to the details, such as cleaning the windows including the frames, dusting baseboards, and washing any white trim (Magic Eraser sponges are fantastic for this task) including light switch plates, doorknobs and dusting the window treatments such as blinds, and any ceiling fan blades. Also, search for spider webs alongside the ceilings and make sure to check the return registers in the house if you have central A/C and heating - those tend to catch and accumulate a lot of dust.

3. STAGE YOUR HOME

Staging your home can make it more attractive to potential buyers and help them envision themselves living in the space. The goal of staging is to create a welcoming and comfortable environment that highlights your property's best features and makes it look as spacious as possible. Start depersonalizing it by removing any personal touches, such as family photos, personal collections, or unique decor, which could be a distraction to potential buyers. A neutral atmosphere helps them visualize themselves in the space and imagine making it their own. Next, arrange your furniture in a way that highlights the room's best features, such as a fireplace or a beautiful view. Consider removing bulky or oversized furniture that makes rooms feel cramped. Highlight natural light by opening curtains and blinds to let in natural light, which makes

rooms feel more inviting and spacious. Add some greenery or decorative accessories, such as throw pillows or area rugs, to create a warm and inviting atmosphere (again, think hotels like Marriott, Sheraton, Hyatt, etc.). Make sure to keep your home clean and tidy during the showing process, as doing so elevates your home in the eyes of buyers. Look at pictures online of other homes for sale in your area. The best real estate agents take great care to have their listings appropriately cleaned, tidy and staged. Gather ideas for each room from looking online at photos of your "competition" in the area. In summary, by decluttering and cleaning, depersonalizing, rearranging furniture, highlighting natural light, adding greenery and accessories, and considering professional staging, you can prepare your property to make a great first impression and increase the likelihood of a successful sale in the shortest amount of time, for the highest possible price the market will bear.

4. PRICE IT COMPETITIVELY

The price you set for your property will impact how many potential buyers you attract and ultimately, whether you achieve the highest possible sale price. Pricing your property competitively is essential to attracting the largest number of potential buyers and therefore maximizing its value. However, pricing a property to sell is a complex and tricky task. Even for professional real estate agents, pricing is one of the most difficult aspects of selling real estate. Real estate agents are taught that pricing is both an art and a science. Only the science piece of it can be taught. The art portion of it takes an experienced "eye" and a good "intuition" that is only developed after the extensive experience that comes from being involved in multiple home sales. You must realize that the average real estate agent has taken at a minimum 2 to 3 courses and workshops on how to appropriately price a property. In addition to pricing being a challenging task (objectively speaking) in itself, FSBO sellers are at a disadvantage because they are "too close to the subject" and cannot be as objective as professional agents. Emotions often get in the way when FSBOs are assessing the condition, features, and quality of their home. It is difficult for an owner/seller to switch from viewing their property as a "home" to assessing it as a "house." As a result, the most common mistake that FSBO sellers make is pricing their property too high. There is a mistaken belief that "there is always time to bring the price down." This is absolutely the wrong approach, because the most important period for a new property listed for sale is the initial 10-15 days of going on the market. Overpricing the property from the start wastes the most valuable time a home has to produce the highest price in a sale. An overpriced property will turn off potential buyers and the listing will go stale like old bread. ***Check out the pricing pyramid in the companion guide to this book and how overpricing or underpricing a property impacts the prospect of a sale.*** Overpricing a property could mean the kiss of death and sends the message that you may not know what you are doing. When it comes to selling real estate, going on the market is like dating for a life partner. The longer a property sits on the market (a.k.a. stays single), the more buyers (a.k.a. potential suitors) start to wonder if there is something wrong with it. In the end, a property that sits on the market for much longer than the average "days on market" (DOM) in the area at that time, will require substantial price reductions over time, which will result in a much lower sales price than it could have sold for, had it been competitively priced from the beginning. This is known as "chasing the market" and sellers who fall into this trap end up losing thousands of dollars more than if they had priced it correctly from the start.

Here are some tips on how to price your property:

1) **Research the market:** Research the local real estate market to get an idea of your competition (e.g., research properties for sale in your area that are comparable in size - number of bedrooms, number of bathrooms and square footage). This will help you set a price that is in line with the market and therefore is competitive and attractive to potential buyers. Look not only at properties that are for sale at the same time as yours, but also for properties that sold recently (within no more than 3 to 6 months) in the same area (a radius of not more than 1 mile). Make every effort to go visit in person the homes competing with yours - you will be surprised how much is missed from only looking at photographs, even professionally taken ones.

2) **Consider your property's features and condition:** Consider your property's size, features and condition when setting a price. A property with upgraded appliances or a recent renovation will warrant a higher price than a similar property in need of repairs. Buyers will prefer a "turn key" property over one that would need some work. If your house needs some work, you need to consider that into the price so that you can still attract buyers who will see the advantage of buying at a lower price but having to put "sweat equity" into the house after purchase. An extra bedroom or a bathroom will make a difference in price, even if

the square footage is the same. Also a finished basement vs. an unfinished one. A master bathroom with separate shower and bathtub brings a different weight to the pricing. Same goes for the age of major components that buyers worry about having to replace (roof, furnace, air conditioning, heating, water heater, appliances, etc.), depending on how close they are to the end of their useful life.

3) **Price to sell:** Consider pricing your property slightly below market value to attract more buyers and generate more interest in your property. This may result in multiple offers and a higher sale price. This is particularly important in a shifting market as you must be ahead of the curve to produce a sure sale. Anywhere between 1-3% lower than your competition will make a big difference in how much faster you sell your house than they do theirs. By saving on a seller's agent's commission, you have more room to price ahead of the market. This is also key if the house "needs work." If you don't want to lower the price you may have to invest some money into lifting the house's value to match the price you want to get for it. When doing your research pay attention to what the houses were priced at originally, and how much they actually sold for. Also, overpricing your property only helps your competition sell theirs before yours. ***Check out the pricing pyramid in the companion guide to this book and how overpricing or underpricing a property impacts the prospect of a sale.***

4) **Be realistic:** Set a price that is realistic and aligns with your goals for the sale. While you may have a desired sale price in mind, it

is important to consider whether it is realistic based on the current market and your property's condition.

5) **Get a professional appraisal:** Consider getting a professional appraisal to provide an unbiased assessment of your property's value. This can help you set a competitive price that reflects your property's true market value. Professional appraisers cost around $300-$500 for an appraisal in most parts of the U.S. An appraiser may be extra valuable if you do not have the time to conduct your own research and analysis, or if your area did not have enough recent sales to do a thorough job of comparison, or if your property has very unique features (think "atypical") that make it rather impossible to compare to other houses recently sold in your area.

It does not matter what you paid for your house, or the cost of any updates or repairs you made. The remaining balance of your mortgage does not matter either. What matters is how much are buyers willing to pay for it at the time that you list it for sale. Pricing your property competitively is essential to attracting potential buyers and achieving a successful sale. Further, never underestimate the fact that buyers who realize you are not paying an agent to represent you and you are saving on the seller's agent's commission will expect you to price the home for less. **Unfortunately two people cannot both save the same dollar.** By researching the market, considering your property's features and condition, pricing to sell, being realistic, and getting a professional appraisal, you can set a price that is competitive, attractive to potential buyers, and aligns with your goals for the sale. Finally, to make up for any lack of objectivity you may have as the owner, ask friends or co-workers to review your property pricing and tell you honestly what they think. Choose friends and co-workers who are level headed and who have a good eye for details (as they will need to compare other houses to yours to confirm your pricing).

5. CREATE A MARKETING PLAN

Marketing your property is essential to attracting potential buyers and getting your property sold. We will go over some basics here but make sure to check out Chapter 4 for a more in depth discussion.

Photos: Start by taking high-quality photos of your property, both inside and outside. Real estate agents hire professional photographers who specialize in real estate photography (these photographers have the right equipment for taking photos of homes). A photographer could cost you around $400-$600 depending on the size of your home, the number of pictures, and if they do aerial photos of the exterior with drone technology. Even 3D Matterport tours are becoming a very popular tool for making a home. A Matterport tour can cost around $600-$900 in most parts of the country.

Online Presence: Next, create a listing for your property on various online platforms, such as Zillow, Redfin, FSBO.com, and Realtor.com. Consider using social media platforms, such as Facebook, TikTok or Instagram, to promote your property to your network, and beyond your network via paid advertisements. There are multiple Facebook groups for garage and virtual sales usually sorted out by neighborhood or suburb. Make sure to join those groups in your surrounding areas and list your home in as many of them as possible. Finally, do not fall into the trap of believing that getting on the <u>Multiple Listing Service (MLS)</u> by paying a small flat fee to some brokerage offering this limited service will be enough to market your property. Nowadays real estate professionals do not only rely on the MLS. The best agents out there will do many of the marketing activities listed above in addition to having the property listed on the MLS. Depending on the price point of the property many agents will even pay for Facebook and Google advertising to promote the listing and reach the highest possible number of potential buyers.

Flyers and Brochures: Consider creating and distributing flyers or brochures that highlight your property's best features in all business and places with high volumes of public traffic. Check with your local grocery stores, the library, dog parks, coffee shops, etc., for neighborhood billboards.

Open Houses: Open houses are a great opportunity to advertise your home and meet potential buyers. Hold them at least once every weekend and for at least 2-3 hours. Prepare the house as if there was a showing and make sure to promote the open house dates and times as much as possible throughout the week leading up to the open house.

6. SHOWINGS AND NEGOTIATIONS

When selling your property as a FSBO, it is important to not only be prepared for showings but also to make the house available for showings as much as possible. It is a good idea to obtain a phone number specific for buyers to call you. Be mindful to not list your own personal phone number as it will most likely be displayed on the internet and you will become a target for marketers. Also, many businesses and people can figure out a lot of your personal information via your phone number. In addition, do not list an email as your contact information unless you plan to check that inbox at least once every hour. Additionally, be prepared for negotiations and if you are in contact with a buyer's agent, please be mindful that you are dealing with a professional and you would be wise to conduct yourself with the same level of professionalism. Make sure your home is clean and tidy before each showing and be prepared to answer any questions potential buyers and their agents may ask. ***There are two helpful checklists to help you prepare for this in the companion guide to this book.*** Also, be prepared to negotiate with potential buyers, including the price and any other terms of the sale such as earnest money, closing date, possession date, financing terms, etc. Remember, the goal is to sell your property and move on to your next chapter, so be open to negotiation and compromise. The two biggest mistakes FSBOs sellers make are: (1) they do not return calls diligently and/or communicate poorly and (2) become difficult or play "hard to get" or "uninterested" during the negotiation process. Be prompt to return messages and be clear and specific in your communications. Lack of clarity and vagueness in your communications makes you look unprofessional and untrustworthy, both of which will send buyers and their agents running for the hills and not want to deal with you (no matter how nice you think your house is, there is no house out there that is worth dealing with a difficult seller). Finally, playing "hard to get" or "uninterested in selling," makes you look ...(are you ready for some tough love?) FOOLISH. You put the house on the market, you want to sell it, it is obvious, trust me when I say you are not fooling anyone. Most buyers and their agents will not

believe you if you are saying that you are only "testing" the market. Nobody goes through the trouble of listing a home for sale when they don't have a serious interest in selling.

7. CONCLUSION

Preparing your property for sale as a FSBO is an essential step in the sales process. By taking the time to clean and declutter your home, making the necessary repairs and improvements, staging your home, pricing your property appropriately, creating a marketing plan, and being prepared for showings and negotiations, you can increase your chances of selling your home for the highest price in the shortest amount of time.

CHAPTER 3 - UNDERSTANDING THE LEGAL REQUIREMENTS OF SELLING REAL ESTATE

1. LEGAL CONSIDERATIONS: STATE AND LOCAL REGULATIONS IN REAL ESTATE SALES

DISCLAIMER: Each state and local jurisdiction (e.g., county, village, city, etc.) has its own laws and regulations related to real estate sales, and it is essential to understand and comply with these rules to avoid legal issues and ensure a successful sale. For this reason, this chapter will cover this topic only in general terms.

Navigating state and local regulations related to real estate sales is an important aspect for those selling their property as a for sale by owner (FSBO).

IMPORTANT NOTE: As a FSBO it is your responsibility and duty to research the laws and regulations of your state and county applicable to real estate transactions. FSBOs who fail to familiarize themselves thoroughly with the rules they need to follow are asking for trouble.

Selling a property as a FSBO can have legal implications, and it is essential to understand the legal aspects of the process. First and foremost, make sure you have a solid understanding of the laws and regulations governing real estate sales in your area. Depending on your location, you may be required to complete specific disclosures, such as a seller property disclosure, radon disclosure, or lead paint disclosure, among others as discussed further below. It is essential to disclose any <u>known</u> issues with the property to potential buyers, as failing to do so can result in legal action. Additionally, it is important to ensure that your property's title is clear and that there are no outstanding liens or legal disputes attached to it. A title company can help you find out if your title

is clear for the sale to proceed without issues. Here are some steps you should consider taking to navigate state and local regulations related to real estate sales:

1) **Research regulations:** Research the state and local regulations related to real estate sales in your area. This may include rules related to property disclosure, escrow accounts, title search duties, and the use of real estate agents or attorneys in the sale process. Any online search engine will yield several good articles to get you started and will direct you to the right sources.

2) **Mandatory disclosures:** Research which disclosure forms (Radon, Led-Based Paint, etc.) are required by your state and county that inform of all relevant property information to potential buyers, including any known defects or issues. This can help you avoid legal issues related to nondisclosure or misrepresentation (and prevent buyers from suing you post-sale). Inquire with any local board of real estate agents or your state's association of real estate agents, as they may have resources available to the general public that you can use.

3) **Sales contract:** Make sure to thoroughly read the sales contract you will use and fully understand the terms laid out in the contract. If you use a standard real estate contract, be sure to follow all requirements outlined in the agreement. This may include timelines for inspections and removal of contingencies, as well as specific language required by state or local regulations.

4) **Records of the transaction:** Make sure to keep accurate records of all documents related to the sale, including documents related to the property, inspections, plat of survey,

and escrow accounts. Make sure to scan all originals with all needed signatures and keep a digital copy in addition to the hard copies. This can help you avoid legal issues related to fraud or misrepresentation and if any post sale issues were to arise, you will be prepared to defend yourself.

5) **Professional guidance:** You should seek professional guidance from a real estate attorney or agent who is familiar with the laws and regulations in your area if after doing all the work listed above to familiarize yourself with the local laws and regulations you still don't feel fully confident of your ability to navigate the transaction in a manner that complies with all the rules and will not open you up to litigation. Attorneys and agents can provide guidance on compliance requirements and help you navigate the sale process.

Being knowledgeable of all the state and local regulations related to real estate sales can be complex and overwhelming, but it is an essential part of the FSBO sales process to avoid future legal troubles. By researching regulations, seeking professional guidance, disclosing property information, following contract requirements, and keeping accurate records, you can ensure a successful sale.

2. DOCUMENTATION FOR A SUCCESSFUL SALE

Once you have learned the rules and regulations, the next equally important step you must take is to prepare the necessary documents, forms and contracts with great accuracy. The right documents and contracts will help you protect your interests, comply with regulations,

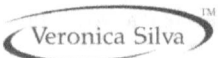

and ensure a problem-free sale. Here are some categories of documents and contracts usually needed for a real estate sale:

1) **Property disclosures:** Provide all necessary disclosures to potential buyers, including information about any known defects, environmental issues, or hazards. Failing to disclose such information can result in legal issues later on. Many real estate associations will have templates available. Search online for your local real estate board and/or your state's association of real estate agents as they may have templates available to the public.

2) **Sales contract or purchase agreement:** Create a purchase agreement that outlines the terms and conditions of the sale, including the purchase price, closing date, and contingencies (financing, inspection, etc.). Make sure to use language that complies with state and local regulations. Many state associations of realtors, or local boards of realtors, will have templates available. Again, check what resources they may have available for the public either online, or at their offices.

3) **Deed:** Prepare a deed that transfers ownership of the property from you to the buyer. This document should include a legal description of the property and should be signed and notarized. In most states the title company will manage this part of the process. Also, title companies sometimes may not deal with owners directly and will require that you retain an attorney to represent you.

4) **Plat of survey:** In most states you will need to hire a professional to prepare a current Plat of Survey. Many states

require that the seller provide to the buyer a Plat of Survey that was prepared no more than 6 months prior to the sale.

5) **Escrow agreement:** Use an escrow agreement to hold the buyer's deposit (a.k.a. earnest money) until closing. This protects both parties and ensures that the sale is completed as agreed upon.

6) **Closing documents:** Prepare all necessary closing documents, including the settlement statement, which outlines all costs associated with the sale, and the closing disclosure, which provides a breakdown of the loan details. If a real estate attorney is involved, they will help you manage the preparation of these documents.

Preparing the necessary documents and contracts can be overwhelming, but it is a critical step in the FSBO sales process. Most of these documents are gathered and prepared by the attorneys in the transaction and/or the title company. By providing all necessary disclosures, creating a purchase agreement, preparing a deed, using an escrow agreement, and preparing closing documents, you can protect your interests and ensure a successful sale. If in doubt whether you are complying with all state and local rules, it is important that you seek professional guidance, such as a real estate attorney or agent, to ensure that all necessary documents are prepared and comply with state and local regulations.

3. THE ROLE OF ATTORNEYS AND OTHER PROFESSIONALS

Understanding the role of attorneys and other professionals in the sale process is essential for those selling their property as a for sale by

owner (FSBO). While some FSBO sellers choose to manage the sale process on their own, others may choose to seek the guidance of a legal professional to ensure that all aspects of the sale are managed correctly. My personal recommendation is to hire an attorney who only does real estate work (mainly closings), particularly if you are in a state in which most transactions are handled by an attorney. You will find also that Title Companies may refuse to work with you or handle your transaction unless you have an attorney representing you. The cost of hiring an attorney for a closing is well worth it and it is usually only a few hundred dollars. Here are some key considerations when understanding the role of attorneys and other professionals in the sale process:

Attorneys

1) **Legal guidance:** Attorneys can provide legal guidance on all aspects of the sale, including preparing necessary documents and contracts, navigating state and local regulations, and understanding the offer and negotiation process. However, a real estate attorney will not have a comprehensive understanding and sophisticated knowledge of the market like an experienced real estate agent would. The reason for this is that good real estate agents are constantly studying market trends and statistics and have access to insights about transactions in the market from their own experience and the experience of their colleagues at their brokerage. Real estate attorneys do not dedicate time to studying the market conditions in the same way agents do on a daily basis.

2) **Transactional support:** Attorneys can also provide transactional support during the sale process, such as reviewing purchase agreements, managing escrow accounts, and coordinating with other professionals involved in the sale such as the lender and inspector. If you do not have an agent representing you, the attorney will need to be more involved in managing the transaction. FSBOs would be wise to disclose to the attorney they hire that there is no real estate agent representing them. Further, FSBOs should fully discuss with their attorney the extent of any additional services that the attorney will need to provide to make up for the absence of a real estate agent and what cost, if any, would the attorney charge for the extra services. An attorney will also be helpful to keep track of all the deadlines related to the financing if your buyer is getting a mortgage to purchase the property.

3) **Dispute resolution:** In the event of a dispute during the sale process, attorneys can provide guidance and support to help resolve the issue and protect the interests of all parties involved. When a real estate agent is involved, issues that could result in litigation can often be resolved amicably. Attorneys may sometimes have a more adversarial approach to resolving issues during the transaction, while real estate agents are more inclined to seek solutions working together with their clients in an amicable manner that will allow both parties to reach the closing table in the transaction.

4) **Post-sale support:** Even after the sale is complete, attorneys can provide support, such as reviewing closing documents and

addressing any legal issues that may arise after the transfer of title.

Home Inspectors

Usually hired by the buyers to review the property and inform them of any issues. Sometimes, a seller will hire a home inspector to find out all the repairs that will be needed before listing the house for sale in order to have a smooth sales process. When hiring a home inspector, sellers must be aware that it could potentially increase their disclosure obligations. A home inspector will issue a written report with photographs of the items flagged in the inspection. Also, many home inspectors will offer additional services such as radon screening, roof inspection, septic tank inspection, water well inspection, etc. Most home inspectors will make disclaimers that the inspection is limited to items that are readily apparent and that they cannot inspect the inside of walls for example, or the condition of the flooring underneath carpeting.

Appraisers

Usually hired by the mortgage lender, appraisers can also be a valuable resource for FSBOs to figure out the realistic market value of their property. However, FSBOs must keep in mind that appraisers will base their valuation only on past sales. As a result, an appraiser's valuation may be limited and not reflect current market conditions if the market is shifting. By contrast, real estate agents will arrive at a sales price suggestion based not only on past sales, but on current market conditions and upcoming market trends. As a FSBO you will need to meet the appraiser the mortgage lender sends out to view and value your property. Provide all the research you have done to set the price of your home. Don't think the appraiser is your friend. The appraisers work for the buyer's mortgage lender, not you. Keep it professional and be prepared to justify, and defend, the price of your home in the eyes of the appraiser.

Surveyors

Usually hired by the seller or the seller's attorney to draw up the Plat of Survey. Title companies and sometimes the mortgage lender will require this document in order to provide extended insurance coverage for the buyer. In some transactions in states where this is a requirement, a buyer may be willing to waive their right to a recent Plat of Survey.

4. CONCLUSION

Selling a property as a FSBO requires an understanding of the legal and financial aspects of the process. It is essential to ensure that you are in compliance with any and all laws and regulations governing real estate sales in your area, and to be prepared for the negotiation process. By keeping these considerations in mind, you can successfully sell your property as a FSBO. While attorneys and other professionals can be valuable resources for FSBO sellers, it is important to remember that they do come with additional costs. Sellers should consider their budget and the complexity of the sale before deciding to seek professional legal guidance. Additionally, sellers should ensure that any professional they work with is licensed and experienced in real estate transactions in their state or local jurisdiction.

Overall, understanding the role of attorneys and other professionals in the sale process can help FSBO sellers make informed decisions and ensure a smooth sale. Whether a seller chooses to manage the sale process on their own or seek professional guidance, it is essential to ensure that all aspects of the sale comply with state and local laws and regulations and protect the interests of all parties involved.

CHAPTER 4 - MARKETING AND ADVERTISING YOUR PROPERTY

Is your house ready to be shown? Have you completed all the preparation steps outlined in Chapter 2? You would not go on a date with wrinkly clothes, would you? (I surely hope not!) Just as you would not go on dates with wrinkled clothes, you should not begin marketing your property until it's ready for viewing. If you start marketing and showing your property before it is ready, buyers will be turned off and question if the property has been adequately maintained under your ownership if you are presenting it in poor condition or state of disrepair to the people who expect to see it in its best light.

1. COMPREHENSIVE MARKETING PLAN

Once you have prepared your home for sale, it is time to market and advertise your property to attract potential buyers. We briefly discussed marketing in Chapter 2. This chapter will provide further details and key strategies you can use to effectively market and advertise your property. As a FSBO, it is up to you to create a marketing plan and promote your property. Creating a comprehensive marketing plan is essential to attract the largest possible number of potential buyers. A well-crafted marketing plan will be your road map to reach a larger audience and increase the chances of finding the right buyer for your property. Even if you list your property for sale on the Multiple Listing Service (MLS) you are still at a disadvantage compared to real estate agents who, as professionals, have powerful networks and large databases of potential buyers they rely on. As a FSBO, you are not involved in real estate transactions day in and day out like most real estate agents and that is a

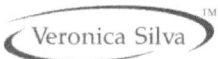

significant disadvantage you must overcome to be a successful FSBO seller.

Here are some key considerations when creating a comprehensive marketing plan:

Define your target audience: Before you begin marketing your property, it is important to define your target audience. Who is most likely to be interested in your property? What are their needs and preferences? Defining your target audience can help you tailor your marketing efforts and increase the chances of reaching potential buyers who are most likely to be interested in your property.

Use a variety of marketing channels: To reach a larger audience, it is important to use a variety of marketing channels, including online listings, social media, print advertising, and even word of mouth. Consider which channels are most likely to reach your target audience and create a marketing plan that leverages those channels effectively. These marketing channels are discussed in more detail later in this chapter.

Highlight key features and benefits: When marketing your property, it is important to highlight its key features and benefits. What makes your property stand out from others on the market? Is it its location, its size, or its unique design? By highlighting these features and benefits, you can help potential buyers see the value in your property and increase their interest in making an offer.

Include high-quality visuals: High-quality visuals, such as *professional* photos and videos, can help showcase your property in the best possible light. Consider hiring a real estate photographer or videographer to create high-quality visuals that will help attract potential buyers. Nowadays, 3D tours made with the popular Matterport camera are all the rage. Depending on your home's price point you may not be able to skip hiring a professional to prepare a 3D tour as they are becoming very popular and not having one will put you at a disadvantage.

Monitor and adjust your marketing plan: Once you have created a marketing plan, it is important to monitor its effectiveness and make adjustments as needed. Consider tracking metrics such as website traffic, leads generated, and offers received, and use that data to adjust your marketing plan and increase its effectiveness.

Overall, creating a comprehensive marketing plan is essential when selling your property as a FSBO. By defining your target audience, using a variety of marketing channels, highlighting key features and benefits, including high-quality visuals, and monitoring and adjusting your plan as needed, you can increase your chances of finding many buyers interested in your property. The more buyers interested in your property you can reach, the more likely the right buyer will place the highest possible offer, and the higher the chances that you will find that buyer in the shortest amount of time.

2. LEVERAGING SOCIAL MEDIA, ONLINE CLASSIFIEDS, AND OTHER PLATFORMS TO PROMOTE YOUR PROPERTY

When selling your property as a for sale by owner (FSBO), leveraging social media, online classifieds, and other platforms can help you reach the largest possible pool of buyers. All the most successful agents are doing it, and so should you. Here are some tips for using these platforms effectively:

1) Social media is a powerful marketing tool that can help you reach a large number of potential buyers in your target audience. Social media platforms such as Facebook, Instagram, TikTok, YouTube, and Twitter can be powerful tools for promoting your property. Consider creating a dedicated page, profile or account for your property, and share photos, videos, and information about your property. You can also rely on these platforms to promote any open houses you plan to hold. You can also consider using paid social media advertising to reach an even larger audience in your target market.

2) Online classifieds such as Craigslist and Kijiji (Canada) can be effective tools for reaching potential buyers in your local area. Be sure to create a compelling listing that highlights the key features and benefits of your property and include high-quality photos and contact information. Be mindful of how you present your listing as sometimes these platforms have been used by con-artists to scam people.

3) There are a variety of real estate listing websites that you can use to promote your property, such as Zillow, FSBO.com, forsalebyowner.com, Trulia, Redfin, etc. These websites can help you reach a larger audience and increase your chances of finding the right buyer. Be sure to create a compelling listing that includes high-quality photos and detailed information about your property. If you have paid a flat fee service to list your property on the MLS, your listing will get automatically syndicated to multiple real estate websites. However, if you are

not listed on the MLS, you will need to create multiple listings, one in each of these websites.

4) Consider joining online forums and groups related to real estate or your local community and use these platforms to promote your property. Be sure to follow the rules of the group and avoid spamming or being overly promotional.

5) In today's digital age, virtual tours are a great way to give potential buyers an immersive and detailed look at your property. Consider creating a virtual tour using 360-degree photos or a 3D video tour that showcases its key features and benefits and share these on social media and other platforms.

6) Consider holding a few open houses (preferably on the weekend) when many people are available to attend. Be sure to prepare your home for the open house by cleaning and decluttering and presenting it just as it was on the day the photos were taken - you want buyers to come in and feel familiar with your property because it looks exactly the same as in the pictures they already saw. You should also consider providing refreshments and creating a welcoming atmosphere.

7) Flyers and postcards are another effective way to market your property. Create a professional-looking flyer or postcard that includes photos and details about your property. Distribute these flyers or postcards in your local area, such as in coffee shops or other public spaces. You can also mail postcards to potential buyers in your area using regular mail or an EDDM (Every Door Direct Mail) service. Real estate agents normally

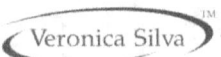
send these flyers and postcards to the entire neighborhood when they first list a home for sale.

8) A for sale sign is a simple and effective way to advertise your property to potential buyers in your local area. Be sure to include your contact information on the sign so that interested buyers can easily get in touch with you. You can also include a QR code on the sign that links to your online listing. Look for a company that can make a sign just like agents in your area place in their listings. It's worth the expense (usually under $100) to look professional and be taken seriously. Please do not just go to the hardware store and purchase a $25-$50 dollar red and white For Sale By Owner sign and please don't just scribble your phone number with a marker on it. First of all, you may stand out with such a sign, but for the wrong reasons. Also, it could potentially send the wrong message to buyers (e.g., if that's what your sign looks like, they will wonder how well (or poorly) you took care of the property while you lived in it!).

9) Local newspapers and magazines are another effective way to advertise your property to potential buyers in your area. Consider placing an ad in your local newspaper or real estate magazine. Be sure to create a compelling ad that highlights your home's best features.

Marketing and advertising your property is an essential part of selling your home as a FSBO. By using a combination of online listings, social media, open houses, flyers, for sale signs, virtual tours, and local newspapers and magazines, you can effectively promote your property to potential buyers. Be sure to create a comprehensive marketing plan and regularly evaluate the effectiveness of your marketing efforts. With a strong marketing strategy, you can increase your chances of attracting potential buyers and securing a successful sale.

3. CREATING EYE-CATCHING PROPERTY LISTING

Regardless of which format you use for distribution, creating eye-catching property listings is crucial when selling your property as a for sale by owner (FSBO). An eye-catching listing can help you attract as many potential buyers as possible and showcase your property's best features. Here are some tips for creating effective property listings:

1) High-quality photos can help you showcase your property's best features and make a strong first impression. Consider hiring a professional photographer or using a high-quality camera and a wide lens to take photos of your property.

2) Identify the key features of your property, such as a spacious backyard or a newly renovated kitchen and highlight these in your listing and photographs. Be sure to include specific details and benefits of each feature.

3) Use descriptive language to help potential buyers visualize themselves in your property. For example, instead of simply stating that your property has a large backyard, describe it as a "spacious outdoor oasis that's perfect for entertaining."

4) Be sure to provide detailed information about your property and its location, including square footage* (including the source), number of bedrooms and bathrooms, and any upgrades or renovations that have been made as well as amenities. The more

information you can provide, the easier it will be for potential buyers to make an informed decision. *Important square footage note: Before disclosing the square footage of the property FSBOs would be wise to verify the local real estate rules regarding square footage. In some areas, basement square footage is not counted towards the overall home total square footage, and in other areas it is taken into account only if the basement is a walk-out basement.*

5) Be honest and transparent when creating your property listing. If there are any issues or concerns with your property such as close to a busy road or railroad, it's best to address the issues in your description with a positive spin. This will help you avoid any surprises or disappointments later in the sales process. You will want to avoid potential buyers making an appointment to tour your property, only to turn around a minute after they arrived, and leave because they discovered a feature that was a deal breaker for them. Examples of features that may be deal breakers for some buyers are: proximity to power lines, railroads, train stations, a busy road, schools (pick up lines may be a nightmare for neighbors), no basement, no covered parking, etc.

Overall, creating eye-catching property listings is an important part of selling your property. By using high-quality photos, highlighting key features, using descriptive language, providing detailed information, and being honest and transparent, you can attract the potential buyers that are most likely to want to buy the house from you.

4. CONCLUSION

The marketing of your property begins with the preparatory steps listed in Chapter 2 and includes all the strategies described in this Chapter 4 to reach your target audience of potential buyers. Be thorough and consistent in your efforts. Be mindful to never give the impression that there is lack of planning or lack of care in anything you do to market your home. From the repairs, to the cleanliness of the house (both inside and the curb appeal), as well as the tidiness and the photography or the quality of the brochures print. It all counts. Each marketing decision you have made can send the message that the house is not worth the price you are asking for or that the price is actually a good "deal."

CHAPTER 5 - CONDUCTING PROPERTY TOURS AND OPEN HOUSES

1. TIPS AND BEST PRACTICES FOR CONDUCTING PROPERTY TOURS (PRIVATE SHOWINGS) AND OPEN HOUSES

One of the key components of selling your home as a FSBO is conducting property tours and open houses. These events give potential buyers the opportunity to see your property in person and get a feel for what it would be like to live there. Selling a home is like dating. It is important to make a strong first impression on potential buyers, showcase your property's best features, and create a welcoming and inviting atmosphere. In this chapter, we will cover some of the key strategies you can use to conduct successful property tours and open houses.

1) Before conducting property tours or open houses, be sure to clean and declutter your property. This will help you create a more inviting and spacious atmosphere, and help potential buyers envision themselves living in the space. Although you did this already when preparing the house for sale, you live in that house - clutter happens! That's why you still have to do a little bit of cleaning and tidying up <u>before each showing and open house</u>. The goal should be to always make your property look as clean and decluttered as it did on the day on which professional photos and video tours were taken. Also, make sure to put away and lock all valuables.

2) Any staging done to the property should be maintained during the selling period and even more so the day of open houses and private showings to potential buyers. When potential buyers come to tour the property, they have already seen pictures (and even video tours) online, and therefore, it is important that the house look just like the photographs they have seen online. Most buyers will lose interest in the property if the house looks significantly different from the pictures they already had seen prior to visiting the property in person.

3) Be sure to prepare for potential buyers. This may include printing out property brochures and flyers to be provided to the buyers touring. Also, make sure to have a sign-in sheet for potential buyers to provide their contact information as you should plan to follow up with all potential buyers that you meet. Sometimes people like to attend open houses because they can more easily remain anonymous and when asked to sign in, they will many times provide false contact information. Keep this in mind. For private tours, make sure to keep a log of appointments, and confirm the appointment via phone or email. This is another way to verify that the contact information provided to you was real.

4) It is important to create a schedule that works for both you and potential buyers. Consider holding open houses on weekends when many people are available to attend. You should also be very flexible and willing to work with potential buyers to schedule individual property tours at a time that works for them. You increase your chances of a successful sale when you make

the property broadly available for showings. A very typical mistake FSBOs make is to only offer a few time slots to interested buyers to have access to a private showing. The goal is to make it as easy as possible for potential buyers to come and view the property in person. If you are holding an open house on a specific day, you can try to move all private tours to take place during the open house hour, but don't push it too hard. The most serious buyers usually prefer a private tour as they don't want other people around them when they are trying to get a good feel and look of the house.

5) When conducting property tours or open houses, be sure to create a welcoming and inviting atmosphere. This may include playing soft background music, lighting candles, or setting out fresh flowers (although you ought to be mindful of fragrances that are too strong as many people are sensitive to them or may have allergies). Some sellers go as far as preparing refreshments and light snacks. Offering refreshments is a small but thoughtful gesture that can make potential buyers feel more comfortable in your home. Consider providing water, snacks, or even coffee or tea. This can encourage potential buyers to stay longer and explore your property more thoroughly.

6) It is also important to be a good host. Greet potential buyers with a warm and friendly welcome and be prepared to answer any questions they may have about your property in an informative and objective manner.

7) Without overdoing it, make sure to highlight your home's best features. This includes showing off any upgrades or renovations

you have made to your home, as well as its location and amenities. Be sure to point out any unique features that make your home stand out from the rest. If your property has a fireplace and it is the fall or winter season, it is a great idea to turn the fireplace on for tours and open houses.

8) Be mindful to let potential buyers explore your home at their own pace. Give them the opportunity to walk around and get a feel for what it would be like to live in your home. Be available to answer any questions they may have, but also give them the space to explore on their own. Your valuables and special keepsakes should be packed and put away or locked up. It is also not a bad idea to install security cameras (these days you can find rather inexpensive wireless sets that are very easy to install).

9) During property tours or open houses, be responsive to any questions or concerns potential buyers may have. This can help you build rapport with potential buyers and increase the chances of a successful sale. A common mistake sellers make is to become defensive when questions come up about the property. Answer all questions honestly and politely providing objective answers. If you are unable to answer a question, let interested buyers know that you will find out the information and get back to them later. More details on this topic can be found later in this chapter.

10) Keep a log of everyone who has come by to tour your property, whether in a private tour or at an open house. It is your property, and you have a right to have your own rules on how to collect

the contact information (including a photo of the driver's license) of everyone who will step foot in your house.

11) After conducting property tours or open houses, be sure to follow up with potential buyers to answer any additional questions or concerns they may have. Send them a thank you note or email and provide them with any additional information they may have requested about your property during the tour or open house that you could not answer earlier. This can help keep you at the forefront of their minds and increase the likelihood that they will consider making an offer on your home. Also, it is perfectly valid and a common practice to ask potential buyers for their feedback after they have toured the property. Providing a short list of about 4-5 questions for them to answer about the property works well as it makes it easier for potential buyers to share their thoughts. Open-ended questions as well as specific ones are useful (e.g., What is the best feature of the house? What would you improve about the house? What is your opinion of the price? *Just right, *Too high, *Too low. In summary, communication is key with potential buyers to build rapport and increase the chances of a successful sale. **Look for a sample of a feedback form in the companion guide to this book.**

2. HANDLING QUESTIONS AND OBJECTIONS FROM POTENTIAL BUYERS

Handling questions and objections from potential buyers is an important part of the real estate sales process. Potential buyers may have a variety of questions and concerns, and it is important to be prepared to address these in a professional and informative manner. Here are some tips for handling questions and objections from potential buyers:

1) **Be prepared:** Before showing your property, take the time to put yourself in the buyers' shoes and anticipate any potential objections or concerns that may arise. This will help you be better prepared to address any questions that may arise in an informative manner without getting defensive.

2) **Listen actively:** When a potential buyer has a question or objection, it is important to listen actively and understand their perspective. This will help you respond more effectively in an objective manner and create a positive rapport with potential buyers.

3) **Stay calm and professional:** Even if a potential buyer expresses concern or disagreement, it is important to stay calm and professional. This will help you maintain a positive and productive dialogue and increase the chances of a successful sale. Be mindful of not becoming confrontational or combative.

4) **Provide information and evidence:** If a potential buyer has a question or concern about your property, be prepared to provide information and evidence to support your position. This may include data on recent sales in the area, property inspection reports, or other relevant information.

5) **Address concerns directly:** When a potential buyer expresses a concern or objection, it is important to address it directly and provide a clear and concise response as opposed to being vague and evasive. This will help you build trust and credibility with potential buyers.

6) **Offer solutions:** If a potential buyer has a concern or objection that you are unable to address directly, consider offering potential solutions or alternatives. This can help you maintain a positive dialogue, show your willingness to work things out with a buyer, and increase the chances of a successful sale.

Overall, handling questions and objections from potential buyers is an important part of the real estate sales process. By being prepared, listening actively, staying calm and professional, providing information and evidence, addressing concerns directly, and offering solutions, you can create a positive and productive dialogue with potential buyers and increase the chances of a successful sale.

3. CONCLUSION

Conducting property tours and open houses is an essential part of selling your home as a FSBO. By preparing your home, creating a schedule, being a good host, highlighting your home's best features, letting buyers explore, offering refreshments, and following up with potential buyers, you can increase your chances of attracting interested buyers and making them excited about putting an offer that will lead to securing a successful sale. With these tips, you can conduct property tours and open houses that showcase your home's best qualities and make work to your advantage. Also, when potential buyers feel welcome and comfortable their interest in your property will grow.

CHAPTER 6 - NAVIGATING THE OFFER AND NEGOTIATION PROCESS

1. UNDERSTANDING HOW OFFERS AND NEGOTIATIONS WORK IN REAL ESTATE SALES

Once you have conducted property tours and open houses and attracted potential buyers, you are well positioned to receive an offer (or several if you are in a seller's market). Thus, the next step is to navigate the offer and negotiation process. Understanding how offers and negotiations work is critical for anyone selling real estate, including for sale by owner (FSBO) sellers. Dealing with offers and negotiating the sale is often complex and can be stressful, but with the right knowledge and strategies, you can successfully negotiate a sale that works for both you and the buyer. The negotiation process can be a back-and-forth exchange between you and the buyer, where each party makes offers and counteroffers until a mutually acceptable agreement is reached. It is important to be open to negotiation, keep a professional and polite attitude, and be willing to compromise on some of the terms of the sale. This can help you build a good rapport with the buyer and increase the likelihood of a successful sale. In this chapter, we will cover some key strategies for navigating the offer and negotiation process with confidence as a FSBO.

2. OFFERS

Offers in real estate sales are typically made in writing and include various details such as the purchase price, financing terms, closing date, and other contingencies or conditions attached to the offer. It is not uncommon though for FSBOs to receive informal offers *verbally*. My advice to you is to not fall in the trap of discussing *verbal* offers. Do not start negotiating without having a *written* offer in your hands with all the terms that will be discussed in this chapter. A buyer that is not willing to put in the work of writing an offer on paper, in a formal offer document, may not be that serious of a buyer after all. Even when a buyer is serious about your house, they may start verbal negotiations to get some information and insights about you and what you are willing to accept. Refusing to negotiate *verbal* offers will help you weed out non-serious buyers, and also protect you from revealing too much in the excitement of the moment when an offer is made to you on the spot.

Once you receive an offer, it is important to review it carefully and consider all of the details before making a decision. You may choose to accept the offer, reject it, or make a counteroffer. A counteroffer is a new offer made in response to the buyer's offer, and it typically includes changes to the price and other terms of the sale. The negotiation process continues until both parties reach a mutually acceptable agreement.

Among the terms of an offer that you need to negotiate are:

1) **Price** - Probably the most obvious term people focus on during the negotiation of a real estate transaction. A real estate agent will have access to statistics regarding the average sales price in the area, and what is the average gap between the "listing price" (what a seller is asking when going on the market) and the actual "sales price" (what the property actually sells for). This gap is usually a few percentage points. In a buyer's market properties will most likely sell under the listing price, while in a seller's market properties will sell above the listing price as multiple

offers scenario is common driving the "sales price" higher. Naturally, listing price and actual property value are variable factors. Unfortunately, as a FSBO you do not have access to the vast amount of market sales data real estate agents can easily obtain. That data is very insightful information, so it is important that you negotiate price by being mindful of what you do not know. Be open to discussing with the buyer how you arrived at the list price and how they came up with their offer price.

2) **Earnest Money** - This is a good faith amount (usually about 1% of the purchase price) that is given by the buyer to the seller within 2-5 business days of having come to a full agreement for the sale. Earnest money is tendered after the contract has been signed by both parties, buyer and seller. Earnest money is kept in an "escrow account" by a brokerage if a real estate agent is involved, or by the attorneys. While the transaction is ongoing, the earnest money sits in the escrow account. Nobody has access to the earnest money until either the transaction closes, or the transaction is canceled by either party. For the earnest money to be released from the escrow account, the parties must have reached an agreement by either reaching the end of the sales process and closing the sale successfully or by agreeing to cancel their sales contract before the sale goes through. Earnest money is different from down payment, but it is counted towards the buyer's down payment. Think of earnest money as an advancement of the down payment. If a buyer is making an offer and refuses to offer (and pay) earnest money, take it as a sign that they are not serious about the purchase. If the buyer

changes their mind about buying the property after the purchase agreement has been signed and the earnest money has been deposited in the escrow account, and the attorney-review or option period has expired, the seller may be entitled to keep the earnest money as liquidated damages. How much earnest money should be offered? That is negotiable!

3) **Closing Date and Possession Date** - These are two different concepts. <u>Closing Date</u> is the date on which the transaction will be finalized. This is the date on which title to the property switches from the seller to the buyer and the buyer officially becomes the owner. <u>Possession Date</u> is the date on which the new owner (the buyer) gains access to the property. <u>It is most common for the Closing Date and the Possession Date to be one and the same</u>. However, it is not unheard of for the seller to rent back the property from the buyer (the new owner) for a short period of time after the Closing Date. In these situations, the Possession Date is actually a few days or weeks after the Closing Date. If the buyer is financing the purchase with a mortgage loan, the Closing Date will be in part determined by how soon the mortgage lender can get the loan underwritten and processed. In a cash purchase, the Closing Date can be set much sooner, but still, time must be allowed for the title search to be performed and the Title Company to get their processes fully executed.

4) **Inspection and As Is** - In most states buyers have a right to conduct an inspection of the property. Buying a home As Is, does not mean that the buyer will not have this right to inspect

the property. A buyer purchasing a property As Is only means that following the inspection, the seller will not provide any sort of credit for repairs, or assume the obligation to repair any issues found during the inspection. Following the inspection in a purchase that is done As Is, the buyer will need to make a choice between (i) continuing with the purchase and assume the cost of any repairs flagged by the inspector, or (ii) cancel the contract. If a buyer cancels the contract in a timely manner due to issues discovered during the inspection, the buyer will usually be entitled to receive a refund of the Earnest Money paid. However, *waiving the right to inspection* is different from buying a property *As Is*. In the case of a buyer <u>waiving the right to inspect</u>, there is no inspection taking place during the purchase process. In this case, the buyer will only find out about any potential defects after the closing and after the buyer has taken possession of the property.

5) **Financing** - The purchase agreement will contain clauses detailing the financial terms of the purchase. A purchase could be for cash, or it could be financed with a mortgage loan (or even financed by the owner/seller). In the event of being financed with a mortgage loan, the purchase agreement will detail the terms of the financing. The reason for this is that "financing" is usually a contingency of the purchase. If the buyer fails to secure the loan financing the purchase, and therefore cannot "remove this condition," the sale will fall through, and the buyer will be entitled to receive a refund of the Earnest Money. The financing section in the purchase agreement will

detail the type of loan (Conventional, FHA, VA, etc.) and will also detail the maximum interest rate the buyer agrees to pay, and the amortization period (30 years, 15 years, etc.). It is always a good idea for a seller to request a pre-approval letter from the mortgage lender showing that the buyer is able to obtain the mortgage. FSBOs will be wise to read that pre-approval letter carefully as sometimes lenders will write them with very vague terms and subject to income verification and other conditions. As a FSBO seller you will want to be as certain as possible that the buyer you are about to negotiate an offer with, is actually able to buy your house.

6) **Waivers** - A buyer can waive their rights (under State law) in a real estate purchase. In the event of multiple offers, buyers are more likely to waive their rights to an inspection, or waive their right to make the purchase conditional on the appraisal value matching or exceeding the purchase price offered, for example). Buyers will voluntarily waive certain rights as a way to get ahead of the competition. Be mindful as a seller not to push buyers to waive their rights as it will most likely backfire. Buyers will get nervous if a seller presses them to waive any of their rights. This can cause a buyer to get cold feet after a few days or even weeks. It is very detrimental to a seller to have to re-activate the property for sale after having been in "pending" or "under contract status." This creates a lot of mistrust in future potential buyers.

7) **Taxes** - A seller will provide a credit to the buyer for the portion of property taxes that have already accrued during the time the

seller is the owner on title, but that are not yet payable or due to the county. A typical rate of proration for the property tax credit is 105% of the most recent tax bill. However, this is also a term of the sale that is negotiable. In the event of multiple offers, a seller will have more leverage to negotiate a lower proration rate.

8) **Contingency** - A contingency is a condition that must be met before the sale can be completed, such as a home inspection or the buyer securing financing, or a buyer actually selling another home they own but that they need to sell before being able to buy their next home. Contingencies are common in real estate sales and can be negotiated between the buyer and seller as more fully discussed later in this chapter.

9) **Other Terms** - Depending on the state on which your property is located, there might be other terms that are part of the purchase agreement and may or may not be commonly negotiated in the real estate sale - for example, in termite prone areas, a termite inspection might be a common item in a contract that everyone expects a seller to agree to, and assume the expense of having one done. **Also, please keep in mind that laws and regulations in each state may vary and therefore, some of the contract elements mentioned may not apply or may be done differently.**

Understanding how offers and negotiations work can help you navigate the process more effectively and increase the likelihood of a successful sale. By negotiating a realistic sales price, reviewing offers carefully, being open to negotiation, and seeking professional advice when needed, you can negotiate effectively with potential buyers and secure a successful sale that meets your goals and expectations. Always respond promptly to an offer. Do not procrastinate while negotiating an offer and try to negotiate most terms simultaneously. You do not want the negotiation to drag on for more than a day or two. A common mistake FSBOs make is to take too long to respond during the negotiation process. A potential buyer may have more than one house in which they are interested and if their offer and negotiations with the other property is moving along at a normal pace, that buyer will lose interest in your property just because negotiations with you will feel like they are not progressing. Buyers can be fickle and lose interest or enthusiasm in your property (or any property for that matter) rather quickly.

3. PREPARING COUNTEROFFERS AND HANDLING MULTIPLE OFFERS

Similarly to coming up with a listing price, how to negotiate is one of the aspects of real estate sales in which professional real estate agents focus most of their training. As a FSBO you are at a disadvantage not only because you have not taken the many seminars and classes professional agents take to master their negotiation skills, but you also do not have the experience of having done multiple real estate negotiations. Any experienced agent will tell you that even after being a real estate agent for over a decade, they still continue to refine and hone their negotiation strategies and skills with each additional transaction they manage. Preparing counteroffers and managing multiple offers can be a challenging and complex process, especially for those selling real estate as a for sale by owner (FSBO). Take it one step at a time and remain calm.

Here are some tips on how to manage any offers you receive, including multiple offers and how to respond and prepare counteroffers:

1) **Review each offer carefully**: When multiple offers are presented, it is important to review each offer carefully and assess the terms, price, and other conditions already discussed attached to each offer. You may need to prepare a table or excel spreadsheet lying down all the key terms in order to compare all offers thoroughly.

2) **Consider the offers**: Take the time to consider each offer and decide which one meets more of your goals and expectations. Work through the process of elimination. Discard first the offers that present the most number of items that would need to be worked out.

3) **Prepare counteroffers**: If none of the offers meet your expectations, you can prepare a counteroffer that includes the changes you would like to see in the terms, price, or conditions of the sale. While you could make multiple counter offers in a multiple offer situation, it is very difficult to juggle multiple negotiations at once. My advice is to pick the top two offers you have received and at most negotiate those two simultaneously. If you are negotiating multiple offers simultaneously, it's a good idea to let all buyers know so that they understand that the buyer who can reach a full agreement with you first will win the house.

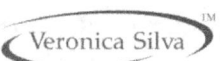
4) **Negotiate effectively:** Negotiate with potential buyers by being clear about your expectations and remaining open to discussion. At this point it's important to let them know what you expect and help buyers meet your wishes. This is not the time to remain secretive. For example, if the most money is absolutely your top goal, let them know that price is of the highest priority. If you are in a pressed timeline, let them know that the soonest possible Closing Date will probably be your preferred choice.

5) **Be timely:** It is important to respond to offers and counteroffers in a timely manner, so that you do not miss out on any opportunities. You will want to find out as soon as possible if you can reach an agreement with a potential buyer. A timely negotiation usually will not take more than a day or two. If you go more than 24-36 hours without a response, you can then consider that the buyer has most likely moved on and/or lost interest in your house. This is even more important if you are dealing with a buyer's agent. This is their job, and they don't sit and wait forever.

6) **Be creative:** Think outside the box. Find out what is of most interest to the buyers. If you are not willing to give in on something the buyers want, work towards finding out what else could be of interest to them that you are willing to compromise on.

Managing multiple offers can be exciting, but it can also be overwhelming. By following these tips and preparing counteroffers that reflect your goals and expectations, you can successfully navigate the offer and negotiation process and achieve a successful sale that meets your needs. It is always a good idea to seek professional advice from a real estate agent or attorney if you have any questions or concerns during the negotiation process.

4. UNDERSTANDING CONTINGENCIES AND HOW TO NAVIGATE THEM SUCCESSFULLY

Understanding contingencies is a crucial part of navigating the real estate sales process, including for sale by owner (FSBO) sales. A contingency is a condition that must be met before the sale can be completed, and they can range from home inspections, to securing financing, to the sale of another property the buyer currently owns. Navigating contingencies successfully is important because it can help you avoid potential issues that could derail the sale too long into the process, or drag you to litigation down the road. Here are some tips on how to navigate contingencies:

1) **Understand the different types of contingencies:** There are various types of contingencies, such as inspection, appraisal, and financing contingencies. It is important to understand each type of contingency and how it could affect the sale including deadlines and how flexible the deadlines that need to be met are - for example, an inspection period or the attorney review period that usually lasts a few business days can be extended per the parties agreement. Likewise, the mortgage loan commitment date can be extended if the underwriters need more time to process the file.

2) **Include contingencies in the contract:** Contingencies should be included in the purchase agreement, and it is important to make sure they are clearly defined.

3) **Review the contingency timeline:** Contingencies typically have a specific timeline by which they must be met. Review the timeline and make sure you understand what needs to be done and by which date. Failing to meet the timeline for the removal of a contingency is the most typical reason that causes a real estate transaction to fall apart and the sale to fall through. As explained earlier in this chapter, the deadlines for removing contingencies can sometimes be adjusted.

4) **Communicate:** Communication is key when navigating contingencies. Stay in touch with the buyer and all other parties in the transaction (attorneys, mortgage lender, appraiser, etc.) and provide updates on the progress of the removal of any contingency impacting your sale.

5) **Be prepared for contingencies not to be met:** Not all contingencies will be met, and it is important to be prepared for that possibility. In some cases, you may need to open negotiations again with the buyer or consider other options. If you had multiple offers, you may have kept another offer as a backup offer and this is the moment when you will need to contact those other buyers to find out if they are still interested and if they can step in.

Navigating contingencies successfully can be challenging, but it is an important part of the real estate sales process. By understanding the different types of contingencies, including them in the contract, reviewing the timeline, communicating with all other parties, and being prepared for contingencies not to be met, you can navigate this process with confidence and increase the likelihood of a successful sale.

5. CONCLUSION

Negotiating a sale can be an emotional process, but it is important to keep your emotions in check. This includes avoiding getting defensive or hostile if a potential buyer makes a lowball offer, and not getting too attached to your asking price or any specific terms of the sale. By keeping a leveled head and focusing on your goals for the sale, you will be better equipped to negotiate effectively and secure a successful deal. Effective communication is key to successful negotiations. Be clear and upfront with potential buyers about your expectations for the sale and provide detailed information about your property and any conditions or contingencies attached to the sale. This can help build trust with potential buyers and increase the likelihood of a successful deal. Navigating the offer and negotiation process can be challenging, and it may be helpful to seek professional advice from a real estate attorney or other qualified professional. They can provide guidance on legal and financial aspects of the sale, and help you negotiate effectively with potential buyers.

CHAPTER 7 - S THE SALE AND TRANSFERRING OWNERSHIP

DISCLAIMER: Each state and local jurisdiction (e.g., county, village, city, etc.) has its own laws and regulations related to real estate sales, and it is essential to understand and comply with these rules to avoid legal issues and ensure a successful sale. For this reason, this chapter will cover this topic only in general terms.

1. UNDERSTANDING THE CLOSING PROCESS AND WHAT TO EXPECT

Congratulations! You have reached an agreement with the buyers!! Now, the actual closing of the sale is the final step in the real estate sales process. It involves a number of steps and requires careful attention to detail in order to ensure a successful sale. Here is what you can expect during the closing process:

1) **Finalize financing:** If the buyer is financing the purchase, the underwriting and full approval of the loan will need to be completed before the closing can take place. This may involve the buyer providing additional documentation or information to the lender. It is important that you as a FSBO stay in close contact with the lender to make sure that the processing of the mortgage is moving along smoothly and that the "clear to close"[1] will be issued on time. Many things can happen during the underwriting process of the mortgage and the sooner you find

---

[1] Clear to Close (or CTC) is the signal from the mortgage lender that everything is ready for the mortgage loan money to be paid out at closing. This CTC is issued once the underwriting process has been completed and all the requirements for financing have been met.

out if there is an issue that will prevent the buyer from obtaining a mortgage, the better off you are.

2) **Review closing documents:** Prior to the closing, both the buyer and seller will need to review and sign a number of documents. These may include the sales contract, mortgage documents, title documents, transfer of the deed, and other relevant paperwork. The title company will usually be willing to guide you and the buyer on which paperwork is needed. Again, hiring an attorney for the closing is usually well worth the expense.

3) **Arrange for a final walkthrough:** The day of, or the day before, the closing, the buyer will typically arrange for a final walkthrough of the property to ensure that it is in the agreed-upon condition. More details on how to prepare for the final walkthrough can be found later in this chapter.

4) **Pay closing costs:** The buyer and seller will be responsible for paying closing costs, which may include fees for title searches, title insurance, attorney fees, buyer's agent commission, county sales taxes, and other expenses. The Settlement Statement discussed earlier in the book will show and allocate the closing costs between seller and buyer. If any credits from buyer to seller or vice versa were agreed upon during the negotiations, you must make sure that any such credits were accurately reflected in the Settlement Agreement.

5) **Transfer ownership and possession:** At the closing, the seller will transfer ownership and possession of the property to the buyer. This will typically involve legal paperwork transferring the

deed and delivery of the house keys. The transfer of ownership is discussed in further detail later in this chapter.

6) **Disburse funds:** At the closing, the buyer will provide funds to cover the purchase price, and the seller will receive payment for the sale of the property. Any mortgage balance owed by the seller will be paid off with the proceeds from the buyer and the buyer's mortgage lender.

7) **Record the transaction:** After the closing, the transaction will be recorded with the relevant county or state office to ensure that the transfer of ownership is properly documented. In some states you will receive the copy of the title recording in the mail.

The closing will be held at a Title Company as they are qualified to manage all the governmental paperwork required to transfer the property title to the buyer. As noted earlier in the book, many title companies will refuse to work directly with homeowners and will require that sellers and buyers hire attorneys to manage the paperwork and navigate the closing process successfully. This will help ensure that all necessary documents are completed, that the transaction is properly recorded, and that all parties are satisfied with the outcome. By understanding the closing process and what to expect, you can help ensure a successful and stress-free sale of your property.

2. PREPARING FOR THE FINAL WALKTHROUGH AND ANY LAST-MINUTE ISSUES

The final walkthrough is an important step in the closing process as it provides the buyer with an opportunity to ensure that the property is in the agreed-upon condition. As a seller, it is important to prepare for the final walkthrough and address any last-minute issues that may arise. The final walkthrough will usually take place on the day of the closing (a few hours prior) or the day before the closing if the closing is scheduled first thing in the morning.

Here are some tips to help you prepare:

1) **Make necessary repairs**: Before the final walkthrough, make any necessary repairs or touch-ups that were agreed upon during the inspection process to ensure that the property is in good condition. This may include cleaning, painting, or fixing any issues that were identified during earlier inspections, or small repairs of damage that may have occurred while the seller was vacating the property.

2) **Provide documentation**: Make sure to have any relevant documentation, such as warranties, receipts, or manuals, available for the buyer to review and keep. If during the inspection process you assumed any repairs, make sure to have a receipt for the work done to show proof it was completed by a professional.

3) **Leave the property clean and empty**: Make sure to remove all personal belongings and ensure that the property is clean and empty for the buyer to conduct the walkthrough. Do not leave personal belongings assuming that they will be useful to the new owner. If there are items that could be of use to the new owner, make sure to inquire and obtain an agreement from the buyer that they will accept any donated items you wish to leave for them. If you do not obtain their permission and agreement, you

risk being asked at the closing table for a last-minute credit to cover the cost of removing any personal items you left behind. Do not forget the outside areas. Clean the garage and mow the lawn. Make sure that as much garbage as possible is taken away in the week before closing. Avoid leaving a pile of garbage at the end of the driveway for the buyers to deal with it.

4) **Keys and Garage Door Remotes:** Make sure to gather all copies of all door keys and label them accordingly. Also, make sure the garage door remotes are functioning properly and have batteries in them (a little courtesy goes a long way). Bring a set of keys and one garage door remote to the title company and leave the rest in the kitchen counter or a drawer.

5) **Address any last-minute issues:** If there are any last-minute issues that arise during the walkthrough, be prepared to address them quickly and professionally. This may involve arranging for repairs, offering a credit or discount, or negotiating a solution that satisfies both parties.

6) **Utilities:** Make sure to set up the closing of all your accounts with the utility companies. It is best to set up the closure of your accounts for the day after the closing date. If you set up the closing for the same day as closing, issues could arise that delay the closing a day or two, and that would cause the utilities to be completely disconnected causing the buyer extra expenses. Avoid the risk of buyers coming back to you for reimbursement for the extra expense. Stop all utilities accounts on the day after the closing to be safe. If the closing gets delayed for several days, you will need to adjust the utilities cutoff date accordingly.

By preparing for the final walkthrough and addressing any last-minute issues, you can help ensure a successful and stress-free closing process. Working with a real estate agent or attorney can also be helpful, as they can guide you through the process and provide valuable advice and support.

3. TRANSFERRING OWNERSHIP OF THE PROPERTY AND COMPLETING THE SALE

Once all contingencies have been met, negotiations have been finalized, and the necessary documents have been signed, it is time to transfer the ownership of the property and complete the sale. The first step in transferring ownership is to obtain a title search and title insurance. A title search is typically ordered as soon as the parties have gone through the inspection process and have agreed to continue with the transaction. The title search will ensure that there are no liens, outstanding mortgages, or other claims on the property that could prevent the transfer of ownership. Title insurance protects the buyer and lender against any issues that may arise after the sale has been completed. The Title Company will be in charge of completing these tasks.

Once the title search and insurance have been obtained, the seller will need to prepare and sign a deed that transfers ownership of the property to the buyer. The deed must be recorded with the county clerk's office to ensure that the transfer is legal and binding. The transfer of the deed and the recording of the new deed will take place on the date of closing at the Title Company. In addition to the deed, other documents may need to be signed and recorded, including a bill of sale, which

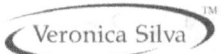

outlines the purchase price and any personal property that is included in the sale, as well as any mortgage documents or promissory notes.

Once all necessary documents have been signed and recorded, the buyer will typically pay the seller the agreed-upon purchase price, either in full or with a down payment and financing arrangements for the remainder. The seller will use the proceeds to pay off any outstanding mortgages or liens on the property and may also be responsible for paying closing costs and other fees. All money exchanges take place on the same day of closing. The seller will also pay any commissions and attorneys fees that were agreed upon.

Finally, the sale is complete once the seller delivers possession of the property to the buyer. This may involve physically handing over the keys or providing access to the property via a garage keypad/code, depending on the terms of the sale (usually possession is delivered on the same day of closing).

Completing the sale can be a complex process, and it is important to work with an experienced professional to ensure that all legal requirements are met, and the transfer of ownership is managed properly. Depending on your location, the closer at the Title Company can fill in the role of the real estate attorney and/or the agent and assist you with the process. With careful planning and attention to detail, the sale of a property can be a successful and rewarding experience for both the buyer and seller.

CHAPTER 8 - DEALING WITH COMMON CHALLENGES AND ISSUES IN FSBO SALES

1. HANDLING DIFFICULT OR UNCOOPERATIVE BUYERS

As a FSBO, you are more likely to encounter buyers who are not working with a real estate professional. This will, sometimes, turn out to be to your own detriment as a seller. Buyers who are not represented by a real estate agent are many times unprepared and, pardon my bluntness, clueless about how to conduct themselves during the process of buying a home. They are often not properly educated by a professional who understands the market and the process of buying a home and will expect you to manage a larger portion of the transaction, meaning that you will need to work twice as hard to keep the sale of your home progressing to a successful result. More often than not, it will feel like you are dealing with difficult or uncooperative buyers. This will certainly be a challenge, but it is important to stay calm and professional throughout the process.

Here are some tips for handling difficult buyers:

1) **Listen to their concerns:** Sometimes, buyers may be difficult because they have legitimate concerns or issues that need to be addressed. Take the time to listen and fully understand their concerns with an open mind and try to find a solution that works for both parties.

2) **Stay calm and professional:** It is important to remain calm and professional, even if the buyer is being difficult or unreasonable.

Responding in a negative or emotional way will only escalate the situation and will prevent both sides from reaching a solution.

3) **Set boundaries:** If the buyer is being unreasonable or demanding, it is important to set boundaries and communicate clearly about what is, and is not, possible. Be firm but polite in your communication and keep things respectful. If a buyer becomes disrespectful or belligerent, it may not be worth it and you must end negotiations. As a FSBO, you will be particularly targeted by some people that may want to take advantage of the situation thinking that you are inexperienced, or do not know much about anything, or that you can easily be outsmarted because there is no professional watching after your interests and protecting you.

4) **Offer solutions:** If the buyer is not satisfied with the property or the terms of the sale, offer alternative solutions that may be more acceptable to them. This could include adjusting the price or offering concessions such as credits. However, if after you compromise on what seems to matter to them, the buyers come up with more demands or open other terms of the sale for re-negotiation, that may be a red flag and a sign that the buyers are looking to take advantage of you.

5) **Work with a mediator:** If the situation becomes particularly difficult or confrontational, consider working with a mediator or a real estate attorney to help facilitate a resolution. This is one of the drawbacks of not working with a real estate agent as they play an important role in keeping the transaction running smoothly helping keep emotions in check.

Remember that everyone benefits when the ultimate goal is to complete the sale of the property in a way that is fair and beneficial to both parties. While it can be frustrating to deal with difficult or uncooperative buyers, maintaining a professional and respectful attitude can help to diffuse the situation, overcome hurdles and lead to a successful outcome.

2. NAVIGATING LOWBALL OFFERS AND OTHER NEGOTIATION CHALLENGES

As a FSBO, you have a target on your back for all the "tire kickers" and other folks who are trying to take advantage of the situation. As a FSBO, you are perceived as more vulnerable because there is nobody there to protect you. As a result, FSBOs receive far more lowball offers than sellers who are represented by a professional agent. You might have heard the saying "two people cannot save the same dollar" which in real estate sales refers to who (seller or buyer) gets to "keep" the dollars not going to pay an agent's commission. Every FSBO is convinced that by going FSBO, they save on real estate agent's commissions. Well, buyers who are interested in transacting with a FSBO also believe that they can benefit from getting a much lower price for the property since the seller does not have to pay commissions to real estate agents, which is the main reason FSBOs receive more lowball offers than other sellers. Navigating lowball offers and other negotiation challenges can be frustrating, but it is important to remain calm and professional throughout the process.

Here are some tips for managing these types of negotiation challenges:

1) **Know your bottom line:** Before entering into any negotiations, it is important that you know your bottom line and are clear as to which terms are non-negotiable for you. This will help you avoid being pressured into making a deal that is not in your best interest. This means that you should fully understand the amount of net proceeds you need to receive from the sale to not find yourself in a short sale situation – which is the scenario where you owe more to your mortgage bank than you receive from the sale of your home. **Net Proceeds** are equal to the sales price, minus all credits, taxes and fees you need to pay to the buyer, the title company, and any professionals you employed during the sale that are paid at closing.

2) **Consider the buyer's perspective:** While lowball offers or other negotiation challenges may be frustrating, it is important to consider the buyer's perspective and why they may be making these types of offers. Perhaps they are trying to negotiate based on certain repairs that need to be made, or they are simply trying to get the best deal possible. Maybe they are convinced that they should be the ones to benefit from you not having to pay commissions to real estate agents - buyers making an offer to a FSBO will most likely believe that they should capture a large part of the saved commissions.

3) **Respond with a counteroffer:** If you receive a lowball offer, respond with a counteroffer that takes into account your bottom line and what you are willing to accept. It is always better to

counter-offer than to simply reject a low ball offer. By sending a counter offer you are letting the buyer know that you are interested in negotiating. This can help start a dialogue and move negotiations forward. It is unwise to not counter an offer. Be mindful that if you counteroffer at the exact same price as the property is listed for sale, you will most likely turn off the buyer who made you an offer and they will move on to the next property. Countering at the same price as it is listed shows a lack of willingness to compromise and unless you have a super desirable property, nobody wants to deal with a difficult, stubborn seller.

4) **Be patient and flexible:** Negotiations can take time and require patience and flexibility. Be open to considering different options and find ways to compromise when possible. However, being patient and flexible does not mean that you should let days go by without answering or getting a response from the buyers. Being flexible is not just about compromising and meeting in the middle. Being flexible also means coming up with creative options and alternatives that may be of interest to the buyers.

5) **Consult with a real estate professional:** If you are struggling with negotiations, consider consulting with a real estate professional or a lawyer who can help you navigate the process and provide valuable advice. Some real estate agents will be willing to engage in the transaction with this limited purpose and charge a flat or fixed fee.

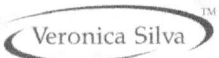

Ultimately, the goal of negotiations is to find a mutually beneficial agreement that meets both parties' needs. While it can be challenging to navigate lowball offers or other negotiation challenges, by staying calm, patient, and professional, you can increase your chances of achieving a successful outcome.

3. MANAGING PAPERWORK AND LEGAL ISSUES THROUGHOUT THE SALES PROCESS

Selling your home as a for sale by owner can be a complex process that involves a lot of paperwork and legal issues. Managing all the necessary documents and ensuring that everything is in order is crucial for a successful sale. Here are some tips for managing paperwork and legal issues throughout the sales process:

1) **Stay organized and keep track of important documents:** Throughout the sales process, there will be many important documents that need to be kept track of, including the purchase agreement, disclosures, and inspection reports. Make sure that you have a system in place for organizing and storing these documents. Use a system that works for you, whether that means a filing cabinet, a cardboard box, a digital folder, or a combination of all of these.

2) **Understand local regulations:** Real estate regulations vary from state to state and even from city to city. It is important to familiarize yourself with the local regulations that govern the sales process in your area and ensure that you are in compliance with all requirements. Make sure to follow all of the legal requirements for selling a property in your state or local area.

This may include obtaining certain inspections or certifications, providing proper disclosures, and following specific procedures for transferring ownership. Make sure that you complete all required disclosures, including those related to lead paint, mold, and other potential hazards.

3) **Consult with professionals when necessary**: If you are unsure about any of the legal issues involved in the sales process, consider consulting with a real estate attorney. They can help you navigate the process and ensure that everything is in order. A real estate attorney can be a valuable resource for managing legal issues throughout the sales process. They can help you draft and review contracts, provide advice on legal issues, and ensure that all paperwork is completed correctly. For the amount of work they do and the peace of mind that they provide, paying a real estate attorney to counsel and protect you in the transaction is most often than not, well worth the fees they charge.

4) **Work with a title company**: A title company can help manage the legal aspects of the sale, including ensuring that the title is clear of any liens or other court ordered restraints preventing the transfer of ownership, and managing the paperwork to execute said transfer of ownership.

5) **Review all documents carefully**: When reviewing documents, take your time and read everything carefully. Make sure that you understand what you are signing and ask questions if you are unsure about anything.

6) **Keep copies of all documents**: It is important to keep copies of all documents that are signed and filed throughout the sales

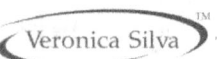

process. It's a good practice to always make multiple copies of signed original documents. This will help you protect your interests and you will be ready to provide documentation in case of any disputes or legal issues that may arise. Particularly the Closing Statement (also called HUD Statement) will come in handy at tax season the following year.

7) **Understand the closing process**: The closing process can be complex, and it is important to understand what to expect. This includes understanding the costs associated with closing, the timeline for completing the process, and any other requirements that need to be met.

By effectively managing paperwork and legal issues throughout the sales process, you can help ensure a successful outcome and avoid any legal or financial complications down the line. Whether you are working with a real estate attorney, a title company, or managing the process on your own, be sure to stay organized and attentive to all of the details to make the process as smooth as possible.

CHAPTER 9 - WHEN TO CONSIDER WORKING WITH A REAL ESTATE AGENT

1. UNDERSTANDING WHEN WORKING WITH A REAL ESTATE AGENT MIGHT BE BENEFICIAL

For sale by owner (FSBO) is a popular option for homeowners who want to sell their property without a real estate agent. Selling a property as a for sale by owner can be a great way to save money on commission fees, but it can also come with some challenges. For those who are not familiar with the real estate market or the real estate selling process, or for those who do not have the time to manage the sale on their own, working with an agent might be beneficial. In this chapter, we will discuss when it is appropriate to work with a real estate agent and how to find the right agent for your needs.

One of the main reasons people choose to sell their property as an FSBO is to save money on commissions. Real estate agents typically charge a commission of 2 - 9% in total of the sale price of the property. While the commission percentage is negotiable, it can still be a significant expense. However, there are instances where working with an agent can actually save you money.

Here are some reasons why working with a real estate agent may be the right thing to do for you:

1) Real estate agents have the experience and expertise to navigate the complex real estate market. They have a thorough understanding of the current market conditions and can help you price your property appropriately. They can also provide

valuable insights into what buyers in your local area are looking for and how to make your property more attractive to potential buyers.

2) Real estate agents have access to a range of marketing and advertising tools that can help get your property in front of more potential buyers. They can list your property on popular real estate websites, create eye-catching property listings, and promote your property on social media platforms. This helps you sell your property faster and at a higher price. They also have direct access to a wide network of other agents, each of them in direct communication with their clients who are active buyers in your local market.

3) Negotiating a real estate deal can be a challenging and stressful process, especially if you are not familiar with the market and you do not have experience with multiple real estate transactions in your past. A real estate agent can manage negotiations on your behalf and can help you get the best possible deal.

4) Real estate transactions involve a lot of legal paperwork and can be complicated. A real estate agent can help you navigate the legal issues involved in the sales process and ensure that all the necessary paperwork is completed correctly. They also make sure that everyone in the transaction completes their tasks in a timely manner. There are many pieces in a real estate transaction that need to come together like a puzzle for a successful closing. Real estate agents are instrumental in making sure that all those pieces of the puzzle do indeed find their way to their final

placement in an organized and expeditious manner meeting the deadlines.

5) Selling a property can be a time-consuming and demanding process. Working with a real estate agent can help you save time and effort by handling many of the tasks involved in the sales process. Most sellers greatly underestimate this aspect. You must think of dedicating about 6-10 hours a week to the marketing of your property as well as managing showing appointments, open houses, and following up with potential buyers and their mortgage lenders. While in the process of selling a house, most FSBOs find that they need to stop doing certain things in their daily lives like going to the gym or visiting with family and friends in order to have the time needed to perform all the tasks required for the sales process.

6) Agents have access to a larger network of potential buyers, and other agents. This can help your property reach a broader audience. Real estate agents can tap into their network to help sell your property more quickly. They can also provide valuable insights into the local real estate market and the types of properties that are in demand.

7) Another instance where working with an agent can be beneficial is when you are selling a luxury property. Luxury properties require a unique marketing approach that most homeowners do not have the expertise to manage. An experienced agent can create a custom marketing plan that will appeal to the right buyers and help you sell your property at a higher price. There

are specialty courses some agents take in order to be qualified to market luxury properties.

While working with a real estate agent can be beneficial, it is important to choose the right agent for your needs. Look for an agent with a proven track record, effective communication skills, and a strong knowledge of the local real estate market. If you do decide to work with an agent, it is important to establish clear expectations upfront. Discuss your goals and preferences and ask for regular updates on the progress of the sale. Additionally, make sure you understand the terms of the listing agreement, including the commission rate and the duration of the listing agreement.

Ultimately, the decision to work with a real estate agent is a personal one. While it is possible to sell your property on your own, an experienced agent can make the process easier and more effective. Consider your goals and needs when deciding whether to work with an agent and choose someone who has the expertise and experience to help you achieve them.

In conclusion, working with a real estate agent can be a good option for those who are not familiar with the real estate market or the real estate selling process. Real estate agents have the experience, expertise, and resources to help you sell your property more quickly and for the best possible price. It is important to choose the right agent for your needs and to ensure that they have a good reputation in the industry.

2. HOW TO FIND A REPUTABLE AND TRUSTWORTHY AGENT

If you have decided to work with a real estate agent to sell your property, it is important to find someone who is reputable, trustworthy, and experienced. Here are some tips to help you find the right agent for your needs:

1) **Research:** Start by asking friends, family members, and colleagues if they have worked with, or have heard of, any agents they would recommend. Word-of-mouth recommendations can be a valuable resource. Once you have a list of potential agents, do some research on their background, experience, and reputation. Start by researching online: look at their websites, read their reviews and ratings, and check their social media profiles. Look for online reviews and ratings from past clients and check their licensing and disciplinary history.

2) **Interview several agents:** Don't settle on the first agent you meet. Interview several to compare their approach, experience, marketing plans, and fees.

3) **Credentials:** Make sure the agent you are considering is licensed and has the necessary credentials to represent you. You can check their license status with your state's real estate or licensing commission. Also, verify their affiliation with a licensed brokerage.

4) **Expertise:** Look for an agent who has experience working with properties similar to yours. Ask for their sales history and the average amount of time it takes them to sell a property. You want an agent who is knowledgeable about the market and has

91

a proven track record of success. When you interview agents, ask them questions about the market. For example, ask them whether at the time of your sale, your local area is in a buyer's, seller's, or balanced market. Another way to ask about what type of market you are in, is by asking what is the current MSI (Month Supply of Inventory) in your area. Other topics to quiz your agent about to figure out how knowledgeable they are is to ask them for supply and demand numbers for your market and property bracket, and for the sales absorption percentages. Ask for references and check online reviews to ensure that they have a track record of success. You should also ask about their marketing strategy and ensure that it aligns with your goals. It is also important to ensure that the agent you choose is licensed and has a good reputation in the industry.

5) **Communication:** When you are working with an agent, communication is critical. Make sure the agent you choose is responsive and communicates clearly and frequently. You want someone who will keep you informed and answer your questions throughout the process. They should be easy to get in touch with and quick to respond to your questions and concerns. Inquire about the reports and updates you should expect to receive during the duration of the sales process.

6) **Trust your gut:** When you meet with an agent, trust your instincts. Do you feel comfortable with them? Do they seem knowledgeable and trustworthy? Do not be afraid to interview multiple agents before making a decision. Finally, trust your instincts when choosing an agent. Look for someone who is

professional, honest, and easy to work with. A good agent should make you feel comfortable and confident in their ability to help you sell your home.

7) **Marketing:** A good agent will have a solid marketing strategy to help sell your property quickly and for the best price. Ask them about their marketing plan and how they plan to market your property to get your property seen by as many potential buyers as possible. Look for an agent who is tech-savvy and uses social media and other online platforms to promote listings.

8) **Negotiations:** You want an agent who is a skilled negotiator and can help you navigate the negotiation process to get the best possible deal for your property.

In summary, finding a reputable and trustworthy real estate agent requires some research and due diligence. By following these tips, you can find an agent who will represent your interests and help you sell your property quickly and for the best possible price.

3. WHAT TO EXPECT FROM A REAL ESTATE AGENT IN THE SALES PROCESS

For sale by owner (FSBO) can be a viable option for those who wish to sell their property without involving a real estate agent. However, some sellers may choose to work with an agent to streamline the sales process, get expert advice, and have access to a wider pool of buyers that could lead to a multiple offer situation resulting in a higher selling price. If you are considering working with an agent, it is important to know what to expect from them.

First and foremost, a real estate agent's primary responsibility is to market your property to potential buyers. They will list your property on the Multiple Listing Service (MLS), which is a database of properties for sale that real estate agents have access to. This listing will include details about the property, such as its location, square footage, number of bedrooms and bathrooms, and any special features or amenities. The listings on the MLS get syndicated to hundreds of real estate websites such as Zillow, Trulia, Redfin, etc.

In addition to listing your property on the MLS, an agent will use a variety of marketing strategies to attract potential buyers. This might include holding open houses, advertising in local newspapers or real estate magazines, and utilizing online listing services like Zillow or Trulia with special paid features. They may also use paid advertising on social media and other digital marketing techniques to reach a wider audience.

Once a potential buyer has expressed interest in your property, the agent will manage all communications with them (and their agent if the buyers have an agent representing them). They will schedule property tours, answer any questions the buyer may have, and negotiate offers and counteroffers on your behalf. This can save you a lot of time and stress, as negotiations can be a complicated and time-consuming process. Of course, like in every profession, there are good and not so good real estate agents. It is up to you to figure out who will be a good fit to work with you in the sale of your house.

Here are some things to expect from a real estate agent in the sales process:

1) **Price guidance:** A real estate agent can help you determine the best price for your property based on market conditions, comparable sales, and the condition of your property. They can provide a market analysis to help you understand the current market trends and set not only a realistic price, but also the optimal price that will lead to the most profitable sale for you as a seller. Overpricing a home is the most common mistake that FSBOs make that end up costing them dearly when their house stays longer than average on the market and goes "stale" making it necessary for the seller to do price reductions far lower than what would have been the optimal price. Real estate professionals will have access to data about recent sales in your area, as well as knowledge about market trends and demand. This can help you set a competitive price that will attract potential buyers without undervaluing your property. While nowadays with the Internet the public has access to a lot of information regarding the real estate market, do not be naive to believe that the level of information the public accesses is the same as what professional real estate agents can gather and analyze. There are many paid services that brokerages use (and costs them thousands of dollars per year) to have the most accurate and updated information to understand the real estate market and make educated estimates of the direction in which it is going.

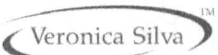

2) **Pre-selling property preparation**: Agents who work with buyers and sellers day in and day out are the most knowledgeable about current market trends and what buyers value the most. When working with an agent, sellers receive insights as to what upgrades are worth investing into in order to produce the best possible sale bringing the highest possible price. An agent helping a seller can easily point out for example that some of the house light fixtures are old and "tired" looking and suggest inexpensive, more modern looking replacements. It is really shocking to many sellers to find out that for a few hundred dollars they can elevate the appeal of their property and easily bring a few thousand dollars more in the sales price.

3) **Marketing expertise**: Agents can create and execute a comprehensive marketing plan to promote your property to potential buyers, including listing it on MLS, creating virtual tours, and leveraging social media, online platforms and their networks.

4) **Networking**: Agents have access to a network of potential buyers and other agents, which can increase exposure for your property to real serious buyers and potentially lead to a faster sale.

5) **Negotiation skills**: Agents are skilled negotiators who can help you navigate offers and counteroffers, contingencies, and other aspects of the sales process to help you get the best possible deal.

6) **Document preparation**: Agents can help you navigate contractual issues related to the sales process, including preparing necessary documents and contracts. They can review

contracts and paperwork to ensure that everything is in order and help you understand any industry jargon or technical terms. They can also recommend trusted attorneys, home inspectors, and other professionals who can help you complete the sale smoothly.

7) **Communication:** A good agent will keep you informed and up to date on the progress of your sale, as well as respond promptly to your questions and concerns. The best agents are skilled communicators who have acquired negotiation skills that can help you save a deal when everyone else is giving up.

8) **Problem-solving and emotional support:** Real estate transactions can be complex, and unexpected issues may arise. A good agent can help you navigate any challenges that arise and find solutions to keep the sales process moving forward. An agent can provide emotional support and guidance throughout the sales process. Selling a home can be a stressful and emotional experience, but an experienced agent can help you stay focused and grounded. They can answer any questions you may have and provide reassurance and encouragement when you need it most.

Finally, when selecting an agent, it is important to choose someone who is reputable, experienced, and trustworthy. It is also important to interview agents before hiring them to ensure that you are comfortable with their approach and communication style. Remember, the agent you choose will be your partner throughout the sales process, so it is important to find someone you trust and feel comfortable working with.

In summary, working with a real estate agent can provide a number of benefits for those looking to sell their property. An agent can provide expert marketing and pricing advice, handle negotiations and paperwork, and provide emotional support throughout the sales process. By choosing the right agent, you can ensure that your property sale goes smoothly and successfully.

CHAPTER 10 - KEY TAKEAWAYS AND FINAL THOUGHTS

1. SUMMARIZING THE KEY LEARNINGS AND TAKEAWAYS FROM THIS BOOK

Selling real estate as a for sale by owner can be a challenging process, but with the right knowledge and resources, it can also be a rewarding one. This book for selling real estate as a for sale by owner has provided readers with general information for understanding the process of selling their property without the assistance of a real estate agent. Throughout the book, we have covered topics such as assessing your property's condition, pricing competitively, creating a comprehensive marketing plan, and navigating state and local regulations. We have also discussed the importance of understanding the offer and negotiation process, including how to prepare counteroffers, manage multiple offers, and navigate contingencies successfully. Additionally, we have covered best practices for conducting property tours and open houses, as well as preparing for showings and managing difficult or uncooperative buyers.

One of the most important takeaways from this book is that understanding the local market and pricing your property competitively are crucial. By doing your research and understanding what buyers in your area are looking for, you can position your property for success and attract the right buyers.

Another key takeaway is the importance of effective marketing and advertising. From leveraging social media to creating eye-catching property listings and conducting open houses, there are a variety of strategies you can use to attract potential buyers and showcase your property's best features.

Navigating the negotiation process can also be a challenge, but by understanding contingencies and preparing counteroffers, you can ensure that you are getting the best deal possible. It is also important to be prepared for difficult or uncooperative buyers and to have a clear understanding of the closing process and what to expect. Whether you are managing these issues on your own or working with a real estate agent, or a real estate attorney, it is important to be organized and stay on top of all the necessary documentation.

This book has also touched on the potential benefits of working with a real estate agent, and how to find a reputable and trustworthy agent to assist in the sales process.

Ultimately, the key to a successful FSBO transaction is having the right knowledge and resources at your disposal. By leveraging the strategies and best practices outlined in this book, you can position your property for success and achieve a successful sale that meets your needs and goals.

Overall, the book has provided readers with a good understanding of what it would entail to sell their property as a for sale by owner, from the initial preparations to the final closing of the sale. By following the best practices and tips outlined in this book, sellers can be better equipped to navigate the complexities of the real estate sales process and increase their chances of achieving a successful sale.

2. PROVIDING FINAL THOUGHTS AND INSIGHTS FOR SELLERS CONSIDERING THE FSBO ROUTE

After reading this book, you may still be wondering if going the FSBO route is the right decision for you. While there are certainly benefits to taking control of the sales process and potentially saving on real estate agent commissions, it is important to consider the potential challenges and complexities that come with selling a property on your own.

Before making a decision, take the time to evaluate your personal strengths and weaknesses, your comfort level with the sales process, and your knowledge of the real estate market in your area. If you have the time to dedicate to educating yourself and managing the sale and feel confident in your ability to manage the various tasks involved in a real estate sale, from marketing to negotiating to closing, then a FSBO sale may be a good fit for you. However, do not fall into the trap of believing that going the FSBO route is easy. While it is not rocket science, it is not effort-free either. Selling a property as a FSBO involves a lot of work and requires a significant time commitment. Relying on proper planning and execution, can make the process manageable and rewarding. On the other hand, if you have limited time or experience in the real estate industry, it may be worth considering working with a reputable real estate agent to help you navigate the sales process. A good agent can provide valuable insights, market expertise, and negotiation skills that can help you achieve your sales goals.

Keep this in mind: only about 8% of homes are sold by the owner. The other 92% of homes are sold by a real estate agent. There is a reason for that - selling by owner is not for everyone.

Ultimately, the key to a successful real estate sale is preparation and planning. Whether you decide to go the FSBO route or work with an agent, be sure to do your research, understand the local market, and take steps to make your property as appealing as possible to potential buyers. One important thing to keep in mind is that a successful FSBO sale requires a proactive and assertive approach. From pricing your property competitively to marketing it effectively, every step of the process requires you to be persistent and strategic. It is also essential to stay organized, keep track of all paperwork, potential buyers, and contracts, and be willing to adapt to changing market conditions. By taking a proactive and strategic approach, you can gain a sense of control over the sales process and potentially save thousands of dollars in commissions.

Whether you are looking to sell your primary residence, a vacation home, or an investment property, a well-executed FSBO sale can be an excellent way to achieve your financial goals and move on to the next chapter of your life. By following the tips and best practices outlined in this book, you have greatly increased your chances of achieving a successful and profitable real estate sale. Remember to be patient, flexible, and responsive to feedback from potential buyers, and be willing to adjust your strategy as needed to achieve your goals. Another important consideration is that working with legal professionals and real estate agents can provide significant value to sellers. While a FSBO sale is entirely possible, it is essential to understand when and where to seek expert guidance. For example, an attorney can help you navigate state and local regulations and ensure that all contracts and documents are legally binding. Similarly, working with a reputable real estate agent can provide you with access to a broad network of potential buyers and help you negotiate the best possible deal.

Selling a property can be a complex and challenging process, but with the right mindset and approach, it can also be a rewarding and fulfilling experience. Good luck with your sale and remember to stay focused on your goals and priorities throughout the process.

3. FINAL WORDS TO TAKE ACTION AND GET STARTED WITH THE FSBO SALES JOURNEY

Congratulations on making it to the end of this book and learning about selling your real estate as a for sale by owner. By now, you should have a solid understanding of what it takes to sell a property on your own and have learned valuable tips and best practices to help you succeed. If you are serious about selling your property as a for sale by owner, now it is time to take action and start your FSBO sales journey. Do not let fear or uncertainty hold you back - with the knowledge and tools you have gained, and the resources available to you, you are more than equipped to take on this challenge. There is no reason you cannot achieve a successful sale and save money in the process.

Remember, the key to success is preparation, strategy, and execution. Take the time to assess your property, research the market, and create a comprehensive marketing plan to attract potential buyers. Additionally, do not forget the importance of legal compliance and documentation. Ensure you have all necessary contracts and paperwork in order to avoid any legal issues down the line. Be patient and persistent, and if you are feeling overwhelmed, consider reaching out to a real estate attorney or other professional for guidance and support. While FSBO

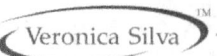

sales can be done entirely on your own, having expert advice can be immensely helpful in some instances. Most importantly, remain optimistic and believe in yourself and your ability to successfully sell your property as a for sale by owner. With the right mindset, approach, and tools, you can achieve your goal and enjoy the financial and personal benefits of a successful sale. Whether you are motivated by financial gain or simply want more control over the sales process, selling your property as a for sale by owner can be a rewarding experience. So what are you waiting for? Put the knowledge you have gained with this book into action and begin your FSBO sales journey today! Good luck!

www.ingramcontent.com/pod-product-compliance
Lightning Source LLC
Chambersburg PA
CBHW062332290526
45794CB00005B/2006